THE

PARENTS AND CHILDREN

PROJECT

THE

PARENTS AND CHILDREN

PROJECT

Raising Kids in Canada Today

GILLIAN RANSON

Rock's
Mills
Press

Published by

Rock's Mills Press

Copyright © 2018 by Gillian Ranson.
Published by arrangement with the author. All rights reserved.

Cover image: Ashley Wiley/iStock

ISBN-13: 978-1-77244-055-3 (paperback)
ISBN-13: 978-1-77244-129-1 (Amazon edition)

Library and Archives Canada Cataloguing in Publication data is available on
request. Contact us at customer.service@rocksmillspress.com.

Contents

Acknowledgements

Books are never solo enterprises, but I am humbled to think of just how many people helped me put this one together. Foremost among them, of course, are the 84 parents across Canada who were willing to share with me their experiences of raising children. They were candid, committed and thoughtful. I am so grateful for their participation, and hope I have done justice to their stories in the pages to follow.

Very special thanks must also go to my friend and colleague, Liza McCoy. Once again, she has listened to my plans, read drafts of every chapter, and made helpful comments. I'm not sure that she knows how highly I value her input and support. This is one more attempt to tell her.

I owe a big intellectual debt to another sociologist friend, Glenda Wall. It was Glenda who introduced me to the field of parenting culture studies in the first place. Her own work, cited throughout this book, has been a model for me to build on. She has been an ongoing source of encouragement.

As well as the people whose stories I write about in the book, I also talked to other parents whose experiences were too difficult to share, but who always made me think, and think again, about all the circumstances shaping family life in Canada. I thank them for their interest in the project, and applaud them for their courage, and the concern and love for their children that shone through in our conversations. Thanks too to the agencies and parent networks that helped spread the word about the project. I haven't named them here for reasons of confidentiality, but they know who they are, and they know how grateful I am to them.

Spreading the word was also the work of the project's website. It was constructed by Kiara Mikita, whose tech savvy, training as a sociologist, and experience as the mother of a three-year-old made her a wonderful resource.

From proposal stage to final production of the book, I have also enjoyed working with Jen Rubio of Rock's Mills Press. Her enthusiasm for the project never faltered; nor did her patience with my quirks and foibles. I have very much appreciated her encouragement and good advice.

Finally, with yet more trumpet fanfares and other family rituals of celebration, I thank Matt and Caro for their sustaining love and support.

THE

PARENTS AND CHILDREN

PROJECT

Introduction

In April 2016 news and social media, in Canada and elsewhere, were alight with a story of a mother in Winnipeg who had received a visit from the province's Child and Family Services (CFS) authority in response to a complaint that her children were playing unsupervised in the backyard of their home.

From the accounts of both the agency and the mother, the CFS worker's visit was a formal one. The worker asked to see the children's sleeping arrangements, and checked whether there was food in the fridge. The mother was asked if either she or her husband were substance abusers, and about the state of the family finances. An official file was opened.

Critical to this story is the fact that the yard in question was fenced in. The children in question were 10 and 5. And the mother in question was inside the house, with her 2-year-old, checking on the older children through the window as she did chores in the kitchen. It was she who broke the story on Facebook. In a post addressed to the "concerned citizen" who made the complaint, she challenged the perception that the children were unsupervised and expressed her concern about the possible official blowback on her family.[1]

The assumption, on anyone's part, that children in these circumstances would be seriously at risk seems unduly alarmist. And that indeed was the general response in the ensuing discussion that surrounded the story. But from another perspective—one also recognized in many of the comments—this situation is only an extreme case of a child-rearing approach that is a radical departure from the practices of most Canadian parents a generation ago. "I remember the good old days when I stayed home as a kid and ran free with my friends from dawn to dusk," said one commentator. "What a bizarre world we live in now . . . where children are not allowed to play road hockey, bounce a basketball in their own driveway or play in their backyard."

It is hard to avoid nostalgic comparisons. Thirty years ago, in another Canadian city, I too watched through the kitchen window as my own children played—in a fenced backyard, with a sandbox and treehouse—and

1

no-one would have alerted any authorities, because that then was what children did. My 6-year-old son walked several blocks to school on his own, and later escorted his younger sister. They played unsupervised in a park near our house, and when they were older, in the river valley just down the hill. I would have described myself as a highly engaged, well-informed, and competent mother, but my mothering did not require the kind of oversight of my children that now appears standard. American sociologist Margaret Nelson has similar recollections. In the introduction to a book tellingly titled *Parenting Out of Control: Anxious Parents in Uncertain Times*, she writes: "In retrospect, and from the vantage point of watching my younger friends and colleagues with their children today, my parenting style seems, if not neglectful, certainly a mite casual. I'm not alone in feeling that something about the parenting of young children has recently shifted in profound ways."[2]

Nelson's use of the term "parenting" is also telling. It is in fact a symbol of the shift in style she is talking about. When she and I were raising our children three decades or so ago, "raising our children" was how we would have described our activities. "Parenting" means something subtly yet powerfully different. It is known in English as a gerund—a noun formed by adding "-ing" to a verb. And that's the grammatical, and sociological, crux of the matter. When "parent" is used as a verb—something that people do, rather than something that they are—there is a shift in thinking about the whole complex of parent-child interactions and relationships. It is a shift that must inform any study of parents and children today.

The Centre for Parenting Culture Studies (CPCS) at the University of Kent in the UK is at the forefront of research examining this shift in focus. In an introduction to a book[3] intended as a primer on the Centre's interests and research in the field, sociologist Ellie Lee starts by noting the relative newness of the term; as one example, books about "parenting" started to appear only in the 1970s, and have rapidly increased in number since then. Lee asks why it is that the language of "parenting"—in "parenting manuals," "parenting classes," or "parenting education"—is now used to talk about any aspect of raising children. A related question, and one that is central to research in this area, is why parents are now understood to be so critical to children's development—and why they now seem to need so much help to bring it about.

This is not to say that parents haven't always been key figures in the raising of children to adulthood, and that, historically, there haven't been experts on hand to give them advice. The argument taken up in parenting culture studies is that parents are now considered to be *solely* responsible; it is, in short, down to parents alone to determine whether their children develop appropriately—as in, happily, healthily, and to their full potential. Sociologist Frank Furedi, whose book *Paranoid Parenting*[4] is foundational to research in this field, calls this *parental determinism*. If children's successful development is all down to parents, it is not hard to understand the accompanying focus (by experts, policy-makers, and politicians, among others) on making sure they get it "right"—and the accompanying assumption that they won't get it right without help. This also assumes that there is some sort of social consensus on what "right" might look like. This consensus is roughly how Lee defines "parenting culture"—the "more or less formalized rules and codes of conduct that have emerged over recent years which reflect this deterministic view of parents and define expectations about how a parent should raise their child."[5]

Much of the research in this field has come from the UK and the US.[6] While there are clearly cultural, economic, and political features that are distinctive to Canadian society, there is also evidence that the deterministic approach identified in research from other countries can be seen in Canada too. (As just one example: the government department responsible for child and family services in my home province of Alberta offers online "tips for parents," beginning with the following statement: "From the time of conception, you as a parent are responsible for what your child experiences in his/her early years . . ." [7])

There are many possible explanations for why this deterministic approach developed, but as Lee explains, one that resonates with many parenting culture researchers is its association with changing ideas about *risk*.[8] These changing ideas play out on a wide variety of social topics, from global warming to the safety of certain foods; risk is conceptualized in many different ways.[9] In the context of parenting, however, it is the *consciousness* of risk that researchers consider to be determinative. Lee cites several features of risk consciousness[10] that contribute to its effect. For example, where once we thought of risk in terms of probabilities that could be rationally calculated, we now think in terms of "possibilities that are untoward"; in other words, bad things that hardly ever happen (what Lee calls the "what ifs of everyday life") are now factored in to our thinking and planning. The classic and often used example of child abduction by strangers illustrates this point. While there is no doubt this is a terrifying crime, statistics show that it rarely happens.[11] Yet parental behaviour now is shaped by this unlikely possibility in a way that would be incomprehensible to earlier generations of parents. Children are supervised to an extent unknown even a few decades ago.

This "what if" thinking leads, according to parenting culture researchers, to a sort of "free-floating anxiety" about society in general. The specific things that parents might once have worried about "have been replaced by a generalized sense that 'society' places children 'at risk.'"[12] This way of thinking has serious consequences. If there is a general social consensus about what might be risky (and what, therefore, children need protection from) we are quick to judge those whom we perceive to be putting their children at risk. (Popular opinion about pregnant women drinking alcohol—another classic example—illustrates the point.)

We use ideas about risk and harm to make judgements that are indirectly but effectively *moral*. This tendency has been vividly demonstrated in a recent study by US researchers.[13] In a series of online surveys using randomly distributed vignettes, they asked participants to gauge the risk to children of different ages left alone in a variety of circumstances—for example, a 10-month-old baby left asleep for 15 minutes in the car in a gym's cool underground parking garage, a 2½-year-old left alone for 20 minutes at home, eating a snack and watching the Disney movie *Frozen*, an 8-year-old left alone for 45 minutes in a coffee shop a block away from her mother. All were circumstances in which, objectively, there ought to have been little risk involved. What varied in the vignettes was the *reason* the parent left the child alone. In every case, when the reason was described as intentional, the assessment of risk to the child was greater than when it was described as unintentional. And within the "intentional" category, risk was gauged to be greater if the reason was a parent's need to relax than if it was related to charity volunteering or work. Overall, mothers' assessments of risk were higher than those of fathers, and much higher than those of childless women and men. One of the study authors was interviewed on the CBC radio program *The Current*. Her comments resonated with the two mothers—both of whom blog about parenting—who were invited to discuss the issue on air. One noted that it was not surprising that mothers were more risk-conscious, since "we are the ones under the microscope, really, always." She added that she had definitely made choices for her children on the basis of how her actions might be interpreted by others.[14]

The problem is that moral judgments get parlayed into formal or informal surveillance, which can start well before there is a baby to be left in a car. As Lee notes, in the US, a pregnant woman's drinking might lead to legal action; in the UK, it could lead to "admonition by health professionals"[15] if she ever got found out. Wherever she lives, it's not hard to imagine the informal social media sanctions her behaviour might also produce—all in the professed interests of protecting her unborn child.

It wasn't always this way. Or rather, it wasn't always this particular "risky" behaviour that might have been seen as a problem in need of a solution. Lee draws on another body of research[16] to explain how it is that issues come to be identified as problems in the first place. Typically, it is a complicated process in which a wide range of actors—potentially including activists, health and educational professionals, celebrities, and the media—make claims about them, using "evidence" that itself may be problematic. Lee contends that in many of the cases she and her colleagues have studied, there is a gap between the consciousness of risk about a behaviour or practice, and the evidence that it is actually "risky." And that is what needs attention. "For example," she writes, "we would suggest this to be true of feeding a baby with formula milk in industrialized countries or drinking alcohol at low levels in pregnancy. The real issue to explain is why formula feeding, or drinking when pregnant, has become so strongly associated with danger when babies born to women who do these things thrive."[17]

Ideas about baby feeding and alcohol consumption during pregnancy are elements of (a particular kind of) *parenting culture*—the "more or less formal rules and codes of conduct" described earlier that govern how parents are expected to raise their children. This version now crosses many borders. To take up the examples just mentioned, in Canada, as elsewhere, the strenuous endorsement of breastfeeding as well as warnings about alcohol consumption at any level during pregnancy are part of public health policy and popular opinion.[18] If they take it seriously, the sort of accountability to which parents are now held can make the job a stressful one—in part, because it is now seen, and felt, to *be* a job. The plethora of parenting manuals, parenting courses, and online parenting resources all offer advice, if not specific training, on the skills needed to do this job—skills that once would have been considered natural, based on common sense, and learned in the normal course of caring for one's children. And as skills, they are geared to outcomes—relating sometimes (in the language of developmental psychology) to what children are expected to achieve, sometimes to the quality of the parent-child relationship.

In the case of babies and preschool children, a key focus of many of those parenting manuals and programs in recent years has been children's brain development. On the basis of interpretations of neuroscience—interpretations that, it should be noted, have themselves been challenged[19]—parents are warned that the early years are a critical window for brain development. They are also warned that parental failure to provide the appropriate stimulation and encouragement during that time can have lasting detrimental effects in their children's later life. UK scholar Jan Macvarish calls this approach "neuroparenting." In her view, it represents the latest addition to the long history of (ever-shifting) advice to parents, "which claims that 'we now know' (by implication, once and for all) how children ought to be raised."[20]

The neuroparenting approach has found its way to Canada too, as sociologist Glenda Wall discovered in her research on Ontario's Early Years Centres.[21] These centres were established as a response to the claims about brain development that had also been picked up in the US. Other provinces have followed suit. Canadian parents, like their UK and US counterparts, are now pressured, first to *learn* how best to provide the necessary stimulating and enriched learning environment for their children—and then to set about providing it.

All of this makes parenting much more stressful. In particular, it makes mothering much more stressful, since mothers are more likely to be primary caregivers to children in their early years. And as US sociologist Sharon Hays pointed out more than 20 years ago, mothers are already stressed enough. Hays identified an approach to mothering that had become "child-centered, expert-guided, emotionally absorbing, labor-intensive, and financially expensive."[22] The term she coined, "intensive mothering," has been widely used to describe the approach that "neuroparenting" only exacerbates.

The risk consciousness described earlier further adds to the stress, by imposing on parents the expectation of constant oversight of *all* their children. In two Canadian provinces (Manitoba and New Brunswick) it is illegal to leave children under the age of 12 at home alone. (This provincial legislation was the reason the Winnipeg mother mentioned earlier received a visit from the authorities.) Ontario's Child and Family Services Act states that a child under the age of 16 may not be left unattended unless provision is made "for his or her supervision and care" that is "reasonable in the circumstances."[23] In the other provinces and territories, age limits are not specified. But it could be argued that they don't need to be; the informal "codes of conduct" regulating parental behaviour are probably effective enough to ensure that the vast majority of elementary-school-aged children in Canada, most of whom live in city neighbourhoods, are never left alone, either at home or in public.

For young children, the greatest casualty of this vigilance is free and unsupervised play—the sort of play my children enjoyed in the neighbourhood park and the river valley. (In a playground not too far from the one they visited there is now a large sign that states: "Playground is designed for children aged 5 to 12. Adult supervision is recommended. Always use playground safely.") This is the sort of play promoted by many scholars, developmental psychologists among them, some of whom also note with concern its disappearance.[24] The loss of free play links to another loss—a connection to the outdoors, and by extension, to nature. Widely cited US writer and naturalist Richard Louv has coined the term "nature deficit disorder" to describe the consequences for children of this loss.[25]

So what has replaced play that is free and unsupervised? One answer is: play that is supervised. Organized "playdates" are now a part of life for most preschoolers and their parents.[26] For many of the children of middle-class parents, structured activities, ranging from team sports to music lessons to art classes—all organized and supervised by adults—are also substitutes. For these same children, living as they do in a digital age that was also unknown to their parents, at least some of their time at home is screen time. Here too, issues of surveillance loom large; for parents, children's vulnerability to virtual strangers, and their exposure to inappropriate online content, are twenty-first century concerns.[27]

Free play is not the only casualty. Fears of surveillance, with consequences like those the Winnipeg mother experienced, set up for parents too a fear of strangers—strangers who are perceived as more likely to judge than to step in and help out. Whether or not it's justified—Furedi's term "paranoid parenting," noted earlier, may be a little strong—one consequence is that parents are increasingly wary of having people they don't know come anywhere near their children. One down-side, according to UK researcher Jennie Bristow,[28] is that contact between adults and children, even in the formal settings (like daycare centres) where they routinely interact, has become highly regulated and circumscribed. Another down-side is that parents' distrust becomes generalized to a reluctance to accept, or ask for, help. Furedi's thought-provoking view is that this constitutes a breakdown of adult solidarity that can only make life for parents more difficult.

The question that must be asked is how well children are served by all this parental concern and supervision. The need for all-powerful parents to protect children from every conceivable risk suggests that children themselves have no agency, and no resources to deal on their own with the ups and downs of daily life. This is a view of children that is also a shift from earlier generations,[29] and one that runs counter to plenty of contemporary evidence of children's resourcefulness, creativity, and ability to learn independently.[30] It is also extremely hard on parents, many of whom are quite aware that "coddled kids" are now emerging as the new professional concern, especially as the "coddling" often extends to adolescence and sometimes beyond. But as researcher Jennie Bristow points out, if parents are now being encouraged to resist the culture of "hyper-parenting" that produces such children, they are still likely to encounter public disapproval when they do.[31] An extreme case in point was the public condemnation poured on American mother Lenore Skenazy when, at his request, and after careful coaching, she allowed her 9-year-old son to ride the New York City subway alone. (The trip was successful, the child was elated about his accomplishment, and Skenazy wrote a newspaper column about it.) She writes that she was labelled "America's worst mom" as a consequence. For her, the experience led to a website, a book, and a new way of thinking about the raising of "free range kids."[32]

Skenazy's focus, reflected in her label, is on the kids. But elsewhere this approach slides into discussions of "free range parenting" which, while certainly offering an alternative to the dominant version, still puts all the onus on parents. American journalist Jennifer Senior suggests a paradox, one that encapsulates much of the foregoing discussion, and also extends it. Senior's paradox is that "modern parenthood" is "all joy and no fun."[33]

Nowhere so far has the joy of parenthood been mentioned. It's what people anticipate when they think about having children, and, at least in some measure, it's what most parents get. But Senior's assertion is that they get it by *being* parents, being present for the "moment-to-moment pleasures" that an ongoing relationship with a child can bring. "How it feels to *be* a parent and how it feels to *do* the quotidian and often arduous task of parenting are two very separate things," she writes.[34] The joy, in other words, comes at a price, which is what most parents *don't* anticipate.

Senior too notes the changes in parenting culture, based on keeping children safe from risk, that make the work of raising children much harder than in the past. But she adds two further reasons why contemporary parenthood may be so challenging. The first is that today's parents, thanks to advances in reproductive technology (notably efficient contraception) can *choose* to have children. This makes a huge difference to how people think about parenthood. Senior writes, "Because so many of us are now avid volunteers for a project in which we were once dutiful conscripts, we have heightened expectations for what children will do for us . . ." [35]

Senior's second reason why parenting is harder today is the changing nature of work. With an explicit focus on middle-class parents, she notes the incursion of work (through digital technology) into home life in a way unknown in pre-internet days. More relevant, because it applies across the board, is the dramatic influx of women with young children into the full-time work force since the 1960s. Figures released by Statistics Canada in May 2016 indicate that among couples in Canada with children younger than 16, the proportion of dual-earners had increased from 36 percent in 1976 to 69 percent in 2015. By 2015, 75 percent of dual-earner couples with children had two full-time working parents. There was also a shift among dual-earner couples with one spouse working part-time. Families with a full-time working husband and a part-time working wife declined from 32 percent to 22 percent as a proportion of all dual-earner couples, from 1976 to 2015. This suggests that during this time, women not only increased their labour market participation, but also their work intensity.[36] Between 1976 and 2015, the employment rate of women whose youngest child was under the age of 6 grew from 32.1 percent to 69.5 percent.[37] If parenting is a challenge in families with two working parents, it is likely to be even more difficult in families where there is only one parent, employed or not. In 2014, lone-parent families accounted for 20 percent of families with children aged less than 16, up from 9 percent in 1976. Lone mothers accounted for 81 percent of them.[38]

Thinking about the balance of family responsibilities and working life that most Canadian families must arrange brings the discussion down to earth, and into the kitchens and bedrooms and backyards of real-life families, of children growing up, and parents trying to do the best they can to make the growing up go well. The expectations, those "more or less formalized rules and codes of conduct" of the dominant parenting culture, loom over all of them, because they *are* dominant. They constitute what parents think they *ought* to do, or at any rate what they know they're expected to do.

As I have suggested earlier, Canada's dominant "parenting culture" appears to share many of the features of parenting in other industrialized countries. But there is also much that is distinctive about Canada—its colonial history, its distinctive francophone presence, its diverse mix of Indigenous, settler, and more recent immigrant populations, its climate, its economy, and its politics, among many other features. These features, too, shape how parenting is expected to be done here. They also shape how it is done in practice. In Canada, as elsewhere, parents don't always do what's expected, sometimes because they don't buy into the expectations, sometimes because they can't, even if they want to. Children don't always do what's expected of them either. They are not passive recipients of parental attention; as noted earlier, they are often more resourceful and resilient, more *capable*, than we give them credit for. So the real story is that other balance—between what's expected of parents and children (and by whom), and what actually happens on the ground.

This is the story I take up in this book. It is, in part, an inquiry into Canada's "parenting culture"—what the dominant expectations about parents and children are in this country compared to others, how these expectations are framed in public policy, education programs, and advice from experts of many kinds, and how they are revealed in public opinion. It also takes account of what life is like for real-life parents, and real-life children, in some of the diverse settings in which Canadian families live.

Two big questions emerge from these separate angles of inquiry. The first asks how well the expectations mesh with the lived experience of actual parents and children. How realistic are they, in the light of the situational challenges and constraints of family life across the country? The second asks, on a more critical note, whether all those expectations are worth fulfilling in the first place. In the context of wide generational fluctuations in understandings of what parents are supposed to *do*, and how children are supposed to *be*, how can we be sure that the current versions are necessarily the best ones?

There are no definitive answers to these questions—at least partly because the inquiry I undertake is necessarily limited by the availability of relevant Canadian data and prior research. But as is often the case, there is value in raising the questions, even if answers aren't forthcoming. I weave the questions through a series of chapters that, while selective in their coverage, touch what I hope are the most important bases.

The two chapters in Part I set the scene by examining the context in which parents in Canada are raising their kids—the "culture of parenting" as it appears from the outside. Part II moves the discussion from the outside to the inside, to the real-life experiences of more than 80 parents across the country, who shared their stories of raising kids in Canada today. Part III is a reflection on all of the earlier chapters, and an assessment of what today's "parenting culture" in Canada is like. It concludes with a look ahead, at the changes that might make a positive difference in the lives of parents.

PART I

Culture and Contexts

The chapters introduced here are intended to describe the "culture of parenting" in Canada from the outside. What *are* the dominant rules and expectations that today's parents face? How do they learn about them? What do they think of them? What difference does the "culture of parenting" make to the ways they go about raising their children?

The first step is to think about how this culture might enter into the everyday life and practices of parents—perhaps through messages from the doctor's office, at a parent-teacher interview, or during a toddlers' play group. Messages also get through to parents via what they are watching or reading online or what is publicized in conventional news media. Chapter 1 explores some of the messages about child-rearing from a wide array of official and unofficial sources.

But the take-up of messages is also affected by the widely diverse family circumstances in which children are being raised. Differences in family structure and culture, parents' work background, numbers and ages of children are among many of the differences that shape parents' ability to respond to the messages—always assuming that's what they want to do in the first place. Chapter 2 looks at some of the settings and circumstances in which parents are raising children—settings and circumstances that might affect how those messages are received.

1

Messages to parents

When I was raising babies in Canada three decades ago, far from all the grandparents and other family members, my main source of information—aside from a kind and supportive family doctor and a couple of friends—was a copy of the famous book of advice to parents, *Baby and Child Care*, by Dr. Benjamin Spock. The first edition of this book was published in 1946. My version was printed in 1979.[1] The seventh edition was printed in 1998, just after Spock's death. At that stage, an estimated 50 million copies had been sold, and the book had been translated into 42 languages.[2] The ninth edition (revised and updated by a co-author) appeared in 2011, to mark the book's 65th anniversary.

That first edition of *Baby and Child Care* brought a dramatic change in thinking about children to parents in North America[3] and around the world. Spock is widely acknowledged to have introduced an era of more relaxed and permissive child-rearing, after many years of advice to parents that leaned much more to schedules, rigid control, and fear of babies being "spoiled." The words of encouragement to parents that opened that first edition (and my 1979 one, too) have become famous: "Trust yourself. You know more than you think you do."

Immersed as I was in the care of my own babies, and without any basis of comparison, I didn't realize the extent of the change Spock's work signalled. I didn't realize, either, that his advice on some topics was not necessarily the same as the advice he had given in previous editions, and that his views would change again in subsequent ones. (My edition had new sections in which he spoke with approval about children having cuddly "comforter" toys like teddy bears—and with qualified approval about mothers' right to paid employment. He wavered between editions on when, and how, toilet training should start. He had more to say about depression in mothers with each new edition.[4] In later editions also his support for mothers who chose to bottle-feed their babies became more qualified.[5]) Credible, respected, and widely read as he was, he was influenced not only by new research findings, but also by the currents of debate that swirled around the child-rearing issues of the day. Times changed, and he changed with them. It's only now, with the opportunity to study advice to parents over the centuries, that I can see his place in the historical order, and appreciate how contingent and changeable advice to parents really is.

Looking at changes in commercially available advice manuals like Spock's is one way to get a sense of changes in thinking over time about children's needs and parents' responsibilities. But advice manuals are not the only source of messages to parents. Sociologist Linda Quirke examined the monthly articles on child-rearing in the popular English-language magazine *Canadian Living* over the years between 1975 and 2001.[6] She found that in the 1970s and early 1980s the focus was on children's health and safety, or on fun activities to keep children entertained and occupied. But by the late 1980s the emphasis was shifting to children's cognitive development, a shift in keeping with the "neuroparenting" trend identified in the introduction. Advice on how to keep children happy gave way to articles about keeping them stimulated—by talking to them, reading to them, and introducing them to new activities.

This shift in focus had implications for parents, and particularly mothers, as sociologist Glenda Wall discovered. She too examined magazine articles—this time in *Today's Parent*, Canada's most widely read parenting magazine.[7] Over two time periods (from 1984 to 1989 and from 2007 to 2010) she noticed a clear change in the way children were represented, and a corresponding change in how motherhood was depicted. In the earlier period (when mothers of preschool children in Canada were entering the workforce in growing numbers) mothers were being reassured about child-care and its benefits to children—who tended to be portrayed as resilient and independent. Mothers' employment was mostly represented as being desirable in the interests of gender equity. Work-family balance was identified as an issue, but the needs of mothers, and couples, were included in the mix.

In the later period, representations of children and mothers reflected the broader focus on children's cognitive development, already noted, but also changed perceptions of risk, as described in the introduction. In this later stage, children were portrayed as more vulnerable, and in need of more supervision and direction. The need both to ensure optimal developmental opportunities for children, and to be vigilant about potential harm, put much more responsibility on mothers in their pursuit of child-care and other activities. "Intensive mothering," described in the introduction, was the expectation. By this time mothers' employment was more of a foregone conclusion. So the challenge reflected in many articles was how mothers might carve out enough time outside of their paid employment to be available to their children. Children's need for intensive mothering tended to displace any recognition that mothers might have needs—for time and leisure—of their own.

My child-rearing days were in that earlier world that Quirke and Wall examined. Articles in *Canadian Living* and *Today's Parent*—along with advice from family doctors, Spock, and a few others—probably represented the range of information about child-rearing available to most parents of my generation. We were the parents, too, who could send children off to walk on their own to school or to play unsupervised in the park without any fear of external judgment.

It's a different world now. The changes described in the introduction—new perspectives on children and their development, changed thinking about risk, the shift to talk of "parenting" as a job requiring skills needing to be taught—have produced a cosmic shift in expectations of parents, and in the amount of information now available to them. And with increasing volumes of information come legions of "experts" willing to give advice. The format of that advice has also shifted. The parenting manuals and magazines of a generation ago have largely been displaced by a digital world of voices clamouring to be heard. Jamie, the father of a 2-year-old, and one of the parents I spoke with for this project, put it well. We had been talking about the sources of information he and his wife consulted (some Facebook posts, interesting blogs and so on). He commented: "It's like an informal network of knowledge that you're always within when it comes to raising kids."

My goal in this chapter is to explore the main messages being delivered to parents in Canada today—the "informal rules and codes of conduct" that make up its "parenting culture." The challenge—and it's a huge one—is to decide which voices to include. Advice has proliferated both from formal sources, like provincial health services, parenting programs offered through local organizations, and other officially sanctioned professional groups, and from informal sources like those Facebook posts and blogs Jamie mentioned. So what follows is a necessarily selective tuning in to both the formal and the informal voices.

The official line

In Canada, as in many other countries, the official messages actually start before a baby is born. For example, "The Sensible Guide to a Healthy Pregnancy," produced by the federal Ministry of Health (Health Canada), contains advice at a high level of detail on topics ranging from prenatal nutrition and physical activity to oral health, smoking, emotional health, and alcohol consumption. (Here, as noted in the introduction, the message is unequivocal. Under "Important facts," pregnant women are told: "There is no safe amount or safe time to drink alcohol during pregnancy or when planning a pregnancy," because "[n]o one knows how much alcohol it takes to harm a developing baby."[8])

Once the baby is born,[9] advice about feeding moves to the forefront. Here, too, the official messages (from the World Health Organization, Health Canada, the Canadian Paediatric Society, Dietitians of Canada, and the Public Health Agency of Canada) are consistent. Parents of newborns anywhere in Canada will hear that their babies should be breastfed exclusively for the first six months, and (once solid foods have been introduced) on an ongoing basis for up to two years (or more).[10]

Health Canada also weighs in on another critical concern for parents of newborns and older babies: how—and where—they should sleep. In a publication tellingly titled *Is Your Child Safe? Sleep Time*,[11] parents are told: "The safest place for your baby to sleep is on his or her back, in a crib, cradle or bassinet." Babies should sleep in the same room as their parents for the first six months, according to Health Canada, but bed-sharing is *not* recommended, for safety reasons. This advice is reproduced on the website of the Public Health Agency of Canada, as part of a Joint Statement on Safe Sleep. The statement, readers are told, "has been developed in collaboration with North American experts in the field of sudden infant deaths, the Canadian Paediatric Society, the Canadian Foundation for the Study of Infant Deaths, the Canadian Institute of Child Health, Health Canada, and the Public Health Agency of Canada, with input from provincial/territorial, national, and regional public health stakeholders from across the country."

Safety concerns guide much more of the official advice, from appropriate car seat use and standards for cribs to the need for helmets for young cyclists. But if physical health and safety must be parents' first concern, they are soon reminded that their children's cognitive development and emotional health are also parental responsibilities. Canada's participation in the multinational take-up of neuroscience findings about early brain development, noted in the introduction, has translated into advice to parents from multiple sources across the country on how they should interact with their children, from babyhood onwards, in order to ensure secure attachment and optimal cognitive development.

The Centre of Excellence for Early Childhood Development and the Strategic Knowledge Cluster on Early Child Development bring a scholarly authority to the job. These university-based organizations, according to their website description, "identify and summarize the best scientific work on early child development," and "disseminate this knowledge to a variety of audiences in formats and languages adapted to their needs." They produce a plethora of brochure-sized publications in a series of "key messages," called "Eyes on parents." One is called "Your child's brain: Building a strong structure."[12] In it, parents are told that their child's brain "develops very quickly" (increasing from 1/4 to 3/4 the weight of an adult brain in the period from birth to age 2; that in the first few years of life "700 new brain connections are made every second"; and that a child whose brain development is healthy will be "more likely" to have a healthy body, show appropriate behaviour, be ready to learn other skills, and control [their] behaviour). Then comes the practical advice. "Stimulate your child's senses," parents are instructed. "Let him experience new sounds, food and objects. This will help develop his senses and build the structure of his brain." Because children's brains are affected by what goes on around them, and their relationships with others, parents are also urged to "play with your child" and to "be a caring parent to your child." Finally, the advice is to "nurture and comfort your child," to "interact with him and be responsive." "Show your child that he can trust you to be supportive and to take care of him when he needs food and comfort."

Advice linking children's brain development to their relationships to others conforms to a new focus, noted by several researchers.[13] Where a decade or two ago the push was to have parents attend directly to how, and what, their children were learning, now they are urged (through a variety of practices mainly boiling down to loving attention) to ensure that their children are securely attached—healthy attachment being seen as the precursor for the emotional capability and resilience necessary for learning to occur. This message too is now shaping Canadian material being made available to parents and service providers. For example sociologist Glenda

Wall, whose work has been noted earlier, found its presence in her analysis of the video series and service providers' handbook that accompanied the Healthy Baby/Healthy Brain parenting education campaign, launched in 2012 by the Ontario government-funded Best Start Resource Centre.[14] One of the video segments urges: "Comfort and hold your baby especially when sick, hurt or upset. Be there when your baby is sad, lonely or frightened."

All this advice is worth outlining in some detail because it represents the thinking behind most other officially sanctioned programs focused on young children. A scan of provincial government websites directed to parents shows a concerted push to have them take the "early years" seriously, with a combination of online advice (often with extensive downloadable publications), and information about programs designed to provide the necessary parental training for the task. The first item on a British Columbia website headed "How parents can support their young children" is a video titled "Why are the early years a smart investment?"[15] (The reasons all relate to the "windows of opportunity" offered during the preschool years, which are "the most active period of brain development"—the video informs viewers that "a 3-year-old's brain is twice as active as an adult's"). Manitoba's "Healthy Child Manitoba" strategy also notes that the early years are "an important time in brain development and a key factor in determining success in later life."[16] A special government website, called ParentZone, tells Manitoba parents: "Parenting may be the toughest *and* the best job you've ever had. From early childhood development to teenage challenges, you'll find resources and information in this website to help you make the best decisions for your family."

Manitoba's approach is typical across the country. Having been urged to take their responsibilities seriously, parents are directed to a variety of community programs and resource centres to inform and support them as they do so. Much of this information and support is delivered through networks of non-profit organizations, funded at least in part by provincial governments, to offer it. Ontario's Early Years centres, and Alberta's Parent Link centres are good examples. There is now a national network of family resource programs, with 500 member organizations claiming to offer services in more than 2,000 communities and reaching more than 500,000 families annually.[17] Much of the programming is directed to preschoolers in the company of their parents, and much of it is informal, with a focus on parent-child interaction and provision of opportunities for parents to network with each other. But outcomes are always borne in mind; early literacy and school readiness inform programming for older preschoolers.

Other influential official sources also offer advice. For example, in June 2017, the Canadian Paediatric Society produced a position statement with guidelines on screen time for preschoolers—in a nutshell, none for children under 2, and less than an hour a day for 2- to 5-year-olds. The statement urged physicians to counsel parents on the "4 Ms" of screen time: "minimizing, mitigating, mindfully using and modeling healthy use of screens." The "modeling" component spoke directly to parents' own use of screens. Specifically, parents were to be counselled to choose healthy alternatives, such as reading, outdoor play, and creative, hands-on activities, and to turn off their devices at home during family time.[18] These guidelines received extensive media coverage. Screen time also featured in a report in November 2017 by researchers representing the Canadian Society for Exercise Physiology; Ottawa's Children's Hospital of Eastern Ontario; and the national non-profit group ParticipACTION, among others. The report,[19] like the position statement just noted, recommended restricting screen time in the interests of increasing the physical activity of babies and toddlers. The recommendations specified 30 minutes of active "tummy time" for babies not yet mobile, and at least three hours a day in a variety of physical activities of any intensity, including energetic play for one- to 2-year-olds. For 3- to 4-year-olds, the recommendation was also for three hours of play, of which one hour should be energetic. One of the researchers interviewed about the report's release noted that only 13 percent of Canadian preschoolers met these guidelines. This report, too, received extensive media coverage.[20]

When children start school, the game changes. Parents, widely described as their children's first teachers, now hand over a big part of the job. But they are strongly urged to stay involved, and to support at home the work children are doing at school. The Alberta government has an interactive website called "My Child's Learning: A Parent Resource," offering parents detailed information about the school curriculum from kindergarten to Grade 12.[21] "We recognize that parents play an important role in shaping the way their children view learning," they are told. "As a parent, you understand more than anyone else how your child learns and processes information. This resource will provide you with a better understanding of Alberta's curriculum and related information for your child. This tool can help you discover what your child is learning, how they're assessed and what resources are available to help them be successful from Kindergarten to Grade 12." In April 2017 the British Columbia Ministry of Education announced the development of an online tool to give parents more information about the performance of their child's school. The news release noted that other potential future uses of the site would be "to make a student's report card and outstanding assignments accessible on a parent's cell phone, as well as a student's attendance history, and school schedule."[22]

Parents of school-age children also continue to be reminded of official concerns about children's health and physical activity. The 2016 ParticipACTION Report Card on physical activity for children and youth[23] was a resounding indictment; only nine percent of Canadian children between the ages of 5 and 17 were reported to be getting the 60 minutes of vigorous physical activity they needed each day, and only 24 percent met the guidelines of no more than two hours of screen time daily. The report card introduced what was reported to be the world's first movement guidelines, and included a tip sheet of advice clearly directed to parents. They were urged to limit children's sedentary behaviour and screen time, to make sure they got the daily 60 minutes of vigorous physical activity (logs of children's activity were suggested), and to be good role models by being more active and less attached to screens themselves. Information from the ParticipACTION report card also received widespread media coverage.

There are also clear official messages for parents about discipline. The *Joint Statement on Physical Punishment of Children and Youth* was developed by a national coalition of organizations facilitated by the Children's Hospital of Eastern Ontario (CHEO). CHEO's website notes: "The evidence is clear and compelling—physical punishment of children and youth plays no useful role in their upbringing and poses only risks to their development. The conclusion is equally compelling—parents should be strongly encouraged to develop alternative and positive approaches to discipline."[24]

All of the foregoing is to say nothing of the advice aimed directly at parents through programs explicitly designed to add to or improve their parenting skills. Most of the parent resource centres mentioned earlier offer programs of one kind or another directed to parents. Echoing the tone of the *Joint Statement*, just noted, the push across the board is for parenting that is *positive*. What that means is described in most detail in the program whose title attests to its focus—Triple P, which stands for Positive

Parenting Program. Core principles include the provision of a "safe and engaging" environment that is also a "positive learning environment"; assertive and consistent discipline (no shouting or spanking); and realistic expectations about children's capabilities. Parental self-care is also a goal.

The Triple P program was developed in Australia at the University of Queensland more than 35 years ago. It began as a home-based intervention program for parents of disruptive preschool-aged children. Over the years it has grown to a highly structured, internationally recognized program offering what its developers call a population-based approach to parenting education. There are multiple levels of support and information depending on parents' needs. The first level (Universal Triple P) is a communications strategy, using electronic and print media of various kinds, to reach "all parents interested in information about parenting and promoting their child's development."[25] Subsequent levels involve group discussions and seminars, and/or personal contact with professional staff, and may be directed at specific child or family problems. Intensity increases, and the focus narrows, with the level of the program.

While specific training might intuitively make sense for parents of children with particular behavioural or health problems or where there might be family disruptions, core parenting skills are specified even at the most basic level. Skill areas range from "parent-child relationship enhancement" (which involves "spending brief quality time," "talking with children," "showing children affection") through "encouraging desirable behaviour" (by giving descriptive praise and nonverbal attention, and providing engaging activities) to "self-regulation" (involving monitoring both children's and the parent's own behavior, and "setting developmentally appropriate goals").

The universal, population-based approach offered by Triple P suggests parallels to other public health measures; it is intended to "inoculate" families across the board against possible future problems. Those invested in parenting education, in Canada as elsewhere, are persuaded that all parents could do with this help.[26] Triple P is now promoted through several provincial governments and offered by many family resource centres across the country. (The provincially supported Parent Link centres in Alberta are in fact required to offer the program in one form or another.)

The burning question, though, has to be the extent to which parents take seriously this, and indeed any other, "official" parenting advice. The outreach figures cited earlier for the network of family resource programs—

more than 500,000 families reached annually in more than 2,000 communities—is in fact a small proportion of the more than 5.8 million families with children counted in the last Canadian census.[27] Perhaps more telling are the statistics on the take-up of parenting programs. A survey published in 2014 of more than 2,000 Canadian parents with at least one child aged between 2 and 12, found that about a quarter had consulted a professional (usually a family physician, pediatrician, or nurse) about a preschool child's behaviour. About a third had asked for advice (usually from a teacher or health professional) about a school-aged child. Only 15 percent had attended a program on child behaviour, child development, or parenting in the previous year. The main reason parents gave for non-attendance was that they weren't aware of the existence of such programs (56 percent)— but 54.3 percent reported that they didn't feel the need.[28]

This finding is not news to parent educators and program developers. Even those involved in the Triple P program note that despite the evidence claimed for its effectiveness, few parents actually participate.[29] Triple P, like other parenting education organizations, now offers its programs online, with a website that opens windows to a highly elaborated set of information and instruction options.[30] The Canadian Association of Family Resource Programs, on a website called *Parents Matter*,[31] has produced an extensive list of online resources for parents also. Indeed, all of the official advice to parents noted so far is available online, and therefore readily accessible to any parent who chooses to seek it out and be guided by it. [32]

There are other clues, beyond program participation, that suggest parents don't always take official advice. (For example, the latest available figures suggest that only about a quarter of Canadian mothers breastfeed exclusively for the recommended six months.[33] About a quarter of Canadian parents still use corporal punishment with their children.[34] And it's probably fair to say that many parents will continue to ignore the ParticipACTION advice to limit their own screen time.) But parents are guided by much more than official advice, however it is distributed. Official advice is part of a much broader social context. It is taken up and commented on and criticized and modified, as other voices chime in with messages of their own. It's hard to escape the conclusion that these unofficial voices may be the louder ones.

Unofficial voices

On January 6, 2017, *Maclean's* magazine, one of Canada's oldest and most widely read news outlets, published an article by journalist Cathy Gulli headlined "The collapse of parenting: Why it's time for parents to grow up." The subheading read: "If anyone can be called the boss in modern, anti-hierarchical parenthood, it's the children."[35] The article was the magazine's cover story for the month. The cover featured a picture of a snarling child holding a pint-sized parent in each fist. The cover caption read: "It's time to stand up to your kids"—and continued (in smaller type)—"Treating children like adults doesn't help them succeed in life. New research shows it's making them anxious, depressed, overweight—and downright unlikeable."

A preview of the article by means of a brief video interview with the author was posted on the *Maclean's* website ahead of its publication, with the message that the story (and the magazine) would be available on tablet and mobile readers "on our brand-new *Maclean's* app" among other sources.[36] Days later, the website noted that the article had "exploded" online, where more than a million people had read it—making it the magazine's most widely read and shared online article ever. A link was posted on *Maclean's* Facebook page, where it attracted scores of comments.[37] Gulli also participated in a live online chat about the article.[38]

The article, along with its dissemination and reception, is a powerful example of change in the way messages about "parenting" now get circulated. It shows, too, what some of the current parental preoccupations might be. The article was based on the 2016 book by American family physician and psychologist Leonard Sax, *The Collapse of Parenting* (the title Gulli later borrowed for her article).[39] The book deals with the tricky issues of hierarchy, rule-setting, and discipline in families. Sax's claim is that giving everyone an equal voice in decision-making, while commendable in other areas of life, doesn't work when it comes to parents and children. His view is that on many matters relating to their children, parents do know best. They do their children a disservice by allowing them choice in areas that actually require adult judgment. Sax calls for the kind of parenting usually defined as authoritative—warm, but firm, with rules about important matters that are not open to negotiation, and that have consequences when breached. And he has suggestions (as the book's cover notes, "the three things you must do") for beleaguered parents to turn things around.

(Sax was also given the opportunity to communicate with Canadian audiences as the second guest in the online chat just noted.)

Sax's pitch to parents to reclaim their authority is reinforced by Canadian psychologist Gordon Neufeld, whose work Sax draws on, and whom Gulli also quotes at some length. Neufeld's concern is framed in terms of children's attachment. Where it ought to be to their parents (from whom they should be learning how to become adults), it is too often transferred to their peers, who know no more about becoming adults than they do themselves. Neufeld, too, has written a book, *Hold on to Your Kids: Why Parents Need to Matter More Than Peers.*[40] (Though this didn't come up in Gulli's article, he also runs a Vancouver-based institute that is registered as a non-profit organization. The institute's website[41] notes that in response to the "growing number" of educators and "helping professionals" who wanted in-depth training in his approach, training courses are offered that now, thanks to the internet, have a global reach. Courses are offered in many languages.) Another Canadian source in Gulli's article was Andrea Loewen Nair, described by Gulli as "a psychotherapist and parenting educator."

The online comments Gulli's article attracted were predictably diverse. There was a lot of agreement with its main argument. "My husband and I have always thought along these lines," said one reader. "Most read article—probably because the problem is rampant," said another. But others took issue both with the argument, and with its implicit judgment of contemporary parents. "It's time that articles like this stop making parents feel like they're failing their children," said one reader. "When you can walk even a minute in my shoes then you have earned an opinion about the job I'm doing as a parent." Another commented: "I'm so tired of seeing these articles about how crappy our parenting is . . . I'm sure every decade can improve on something. Refuse to read any more of these articles."

I use the example of the content, dissemination, and reception of Gulli's article because it shows, in microcosm, the new world of messages to—and about—parents. The article served as the proxy for a book, and Gulli neatly summarized its argument for readers. She also introduced readers to other books—a sign, if one were needed, of the volume of such books now available to parents. They offer advice that is often contradictory, and that may be taken up online by polarized camps of commentators.

An excellent example, which moves the discussion to the parenting of babies and young children, is the work of American pediatrician Dr.

William Sears, the founder of the movement known as attachment parenting. In 2012 Sears too made the cover of a national magazine—in this case the US-based *Time*, whose headline described him as "The man who remade motherhood."[42] The fundamentals of attachment parenting are outlined in *The Baby Book*, which Sears wrote with his wife Martha, a trained nurse. First published in 1992, the book was in print in 18 languages, with more than 1.5 million copies sold when *Time* reported on his work.[43]

It's hard to underestimate the influence of Sears and his family—there are also three physician sons in the attachment parenting "business." And it is indeed a business. Apart from a veritable library of publications, the for-profit "Ask Dr. Sears" website,[44] and a "Wellness Institute" offering certified health coach training, there are also innumerable product endorsements and speaking fees.[45] Sears' reach is global, and Canadian parents are active consumers, of both the products and the advice. There is an Attachment Parenting Canada website and Facebook page, and closed Facebook groups in communities across the country.

The basis of attachment parenting is an understanding that mothers and babies are evolutionarily designed to be close. In practice this means extended breastfeeding (until the baby is ready to be weaned), "wearing" the baby in a sling or wrap to ensure ongoing close physical contact, and having the baby sleep in the parents' bed, or in very close proximity, until s/he is ready for a solo sleeping arrangement. This constant closeness takes care of another fundamental requirement of attachment parenting—babies are never left to cry. While the label is attachment parenting, with fathers and other co-parents encouraged (especially through co-sleeping and baby-wearing) to be actively involved, in practice the main burden is on mothers. And that is the bone of digital and practical contention, in a world where most mothers work outside the home. (It's also not unrelated to the disciplining issue raised by Sax. An implicit extension of his argument is that instant parental response to children's needs may have unforeseen consequences as they get older.)

When it comes to babies and toddlers, it's perhaps the question of getting them to sleep that most clearly divides both experts and parents—in Canada as elsewhere. An alternative to attachment parenting's permissive, baby-centred, no-crying approach is one introduced by another American pediatrician, Dr. Richard Ferber.[46] Ferber's approach is based on the belief that babies, when they're mature enough (usually between 3 and 5 months) need to be taught to fall asleep on their own. Parents are in-structed to develop a warm, loving, consistent bedtime routine, and then put the baby down to sleep while s/he is awake. Babies handled this way will initially cry when they're left. The crux for parents, and the secret, is to leave the baby—initially just a moment or two, and then for longer—be-fore going back to check and comfort. In this way, the argument goes, ba-bies learn to self-soothe and to fall asleep by themselves. Modified versions of this "sleep training" advice appear on popular Canadian parenting sites and other advice sources.[47] For those conditioned to believe that leaving babies to cry is harmful to their psychological well-being, sleep training is highly controversial. Online, the controversy rages.

It also circles around the official line, noted earlier, which points to safety concerns when babies share their parents' bed, and recommends that they share their parents' bedroom only for the first six months or so. Similar circling occurs around other official advice, like that offered on infant feeding. Breastfeeding, as also noted earlier, receives heavy official endorsement, and few would argue that, in itself, it's a bad thing. There are innumerable sources of online support for breastfeeding mothers. But while the benefits of breastfeeding are generally not disputed, there is pushback about the effect such strong endorsement has on mothers who may be unable, or unwilling, to follow through on the recommendations. As the statistics noted earlier indicate, in fact only a small proportion of Canadian mothers actually breastfeed exclusively for the recommended six months. For one thing, it's extremely difficult for mothers employed full-time to maintain it—and few mothers have the freedom (and the fi-nancial resources) to allow them an extended time away from work.[48] But the case is also made online that mothers who are unable to breastfeed exclusively often feel—or are made to feel—they have failed as mothers.[49] There was predictable concern, on social and other news media, about the suicide of a young Vancouver mother late in 2016. The media response followed a Facebook post by her husband which attributed her post-par-tum depression at least in part to breastfeeding difficulties.[50]

US obstetrician Amy Tuteur has written a book, tellingly titled *Push Back*, to register her concern with the activist pressure on mothers in the early stages of child-rearing. In particular, she notes the extent to which mothers are pushed to comply with certain practices (like breastfeed-ing and attachment parenting) purportedly in a baby's best interest, but which, in her view, are being sold more as means to make them feel that they are "good mothers." Tuteur argues that mothers' experience is being valued above what really matters—the outcome for the baby. Breast is not, inevitably, best. (In this context, the US non-profit foundation *Fed is Best*[51] is making the same case. And though official advice on infant feeding in Canada is unequivocal in its recommendations, there is some change elsewhere. In 2016 the American Congress of Obstetricians and Gynecologists amended its official policy to state that "obstetrician–gynecologists and other obstetric care providers should support each woman's informed decision about whether to initiate or continue breastfeeding, recognizing that she is uniquely qualified to decide whether exclusive breastfeeding, mixed feeding, or formula feeding is optimal for her and her infant."[52])

Though issues relating to babies and preschoolers seem to take up more online space, there is plenty of discussion on topics relating to older children as well. In the current era of heightened concern for children's safety, the extent to which they should be allowed some level of free (and hence potentially risky) play was taken up by many media sources following the sobering 2016 ParticipACTION report about children's activity and physical literacy noted earlier.[53] Free play and risk-taking also link to the lively debate about "free range kids," noted in the introduction. The *Free Range Kids* website of founder Lenore Skenazy features a segment produced in 2015 for CBC's *The National* about the phenomenon.[54] The same year Skenazy was interviewed by another national CBC program, which included input from a trio of on-air Canadian commentators and an invitation to parents to voice their opinions through social media. There was also extensive media coverage of Skenazy's visit to British Columbia in early 2017.[55] Canadian parents contribute posts and comments on Skenazy's website. Another subject for parental debate concerns the question of raising "resilient children." Where once "resilience" was studied in children who seemed to be coping in difficult circumstances, now "resilience training" is urged by some parent educators to help insulate children—all children, not just those in serious trouble—against potential risk of all kinds.[56]

Advice and commentary proliferate, on every side of these and other issues. So one challenge for parents is to discern who is talking, and what they might actually know. The Gulli article is worth revisiting on this question also. The article is the vehicle for communicating a message about a particular parenting style—one that is considered harmful to children. But there are messages also in Gulli's choice of sources—the "experts" she draws on for substance and comment. Sax and Neufeld are in the category of highly trained professionals, speaking from professional experience. Two other American sources are cited. Stephen Camarata is a university professor of speech and hearing sciences and psychiatry, and the author of a 2015 book called *The Intuitive Parent: Why the Best Thing for Your Child Is You*.[57] Another is writer Katie Hurley, the author of a 2015 book called *The Happy Kid Handbook: How to Raise Joyful Children in a Stressful World*.[58] (The book's back cover notes that she has a Master of Social Work degree, works as a psychotherapist, and is a "parenting expert.") And then there is Nair, introduced earlier, who is described on her Facebook page[59] as a "parenting educator" from London, Ontario, with more than 45,000 followers.

Nair's credibility as an expert presumably derives at least partly from her professional background—an MA in counselling psychology, and many years of experience as a high school teacher. But she is also a mother, and she uses this background as well in her messages to parents. Her advice is delivered through posts on her own Facebook page and on other sites. "Being Mindful of Your Nice-to-Nag Ratio," published in 2013 and linked in a March 2017, post[60] captures the flavour of her approach. In a 2015 post for the Yummy Mummy Club (about which I will have more to say shortly) she describes how her advice to parents on the need for "positive, clear, firm, concise instructions" to children in challenging situations persuaded her to develop an app,[61] so that her useful phrases could be downloaded to parents' phones. (In that vein, Nair also posted a response to the Gulli article and her role in it. She would have liked a more positive spin, and thought that the key to helping parents to be leaders who still respected their children was not to berate them, but to develop their self-confidence. Her post had eight suggestions to help them to do so, including one that urged them to "choose trusted sources of parenting information."[62])

The "experts" chosen by Gulli, and also by many other media sources—all are popular public commentators on parenting issues—are a sign of change in perceptions of what counts as expertise. Sax and Neufeld, educated to doctoral level in what would seem to be relevant fields, could be seen as carrying on the tradition of writers like Spock, a generation ago. But Nair represents a new category. In an era where "parenting" is seen as a job requiring skills leading to outcomes in children, it follows that "parenting educators" may be needed to provide advice and support, on everything from breastfeeding (call a lactation consultant[63]), to baby-wearing (consult a volunteer baby-wearing educator[64]), to sleep concerns (call a sleep coach[65]). For problems with older children—getting them organized, or managing their screen time, for example—call a parenting coach (who for a fee may offer private counselling, or email advice, or a webinar course[66]). Blog posts on these and many other issues now appear in the online versions of popular parenting magazines like *Today's Parent*, and in the "parenting" section of outlets like the *Huffington Post*. Some are written by people like Nair, who have some professional training to back their advice. But as she herself cautions (in the post just mentioned), dispensers of parenting advice have "a vast range" of training and knowledge; some of what they produce may be far from helpful.

Some, indeed, may have no particular expertise beyond being parents themselves. But legions of them post blogs on personal or group websites, and other social media sites. If nothing else, what they may offer is peer support and encouragement, in virtual communities of like-minded parents. That's where online groups like the Yummy Mummy Club come in. Visitors to its website are told it was founded by a Canadian mother "as a playful place for women to celebrate and commiserate the realities of modern motherhood," and that it has "now grown into a community of like-minded women who spill their stories, secrets and opinions and connect with other moms."[67] (It is worth noting that, though the numbers are far smaller, fathers are also connecting online. As one example, a closed Facebook group of "dad bloggers," started in the US, with members from Canada and around the world, now has more than 1,200 members, and more than 2,800 followers of its public posts.[68])

In the digital world, like-minded parents are able to connect over many issues. One of the mothers interviewed by Gulli reported her involvement in an online baby-wearing group. Gulli comments that "[t]here is no parental concern too obscure not to have an online group devoted to it"—though adherents of attachment parent wouldn't describe baby-wearing as obscure. And it's not just about learning technical tips and getting product questions answered. Group belonging can easily slide into judgment of those who, on the issue in question, are getting it wrong. Parents, in the words of UK scholar Charlotte Faircloth, have become "tribalized."[69] (This even applies to baby-wearing. When the wife of Canadian actor Ryan Reynolds posted a picture on the social networking site Instagram[70] of him wearing their baby daughter in a carrier, there was a rush of responses telling him the baby was not properly positioned.[71] The fact that Reynolds is a celebrity, and considered for that reason to be a parent deserving of attention, is also worth noting.)

The Reynolds Instagram post featured the baby, as well as the father. It illustrates another side to the growing use of social media to post pictures and other information about children. Researchers call this practice "sharenting." They raise concerns about the ethical implications of making information about children public—giving them, in effect, a digital footprint without their knowledge or permission. And while there is also plenty of humour and reality-checking in posts from parents who understand themselves to be far from perfect, there is also a tendency, noticed by both researchers and parents on social media, to post only the positive, to give an impression of advanced children and excessively competent parents which may not represent life on the ground, but which may make others with similar aspirations feel they are falling short.[72] Baby-wearing once again provides an example. The mother in Gulli's article who had joined the baby-wearing group commented: "It's the weirdest site to be on. You see posts and you feel guilty because [parents] are carrying their babies everywhere, doing all these things, having this connection."[73]

This is where the community-building possibilities of online networks can sometimes break down. There are tensions, and there is competitiveness. There is also guilt. The comment by one of Gulli's readers that "this generation of parents is under the microscope more than any other" is telling. Gulli concludes: "That pull and push moms and dads feel—between caring about how other parents are raising their kids while rejecting the constant comparisons—defines this generation of parents for better and worse." The atmosphere of constant moral judgment noted in the introduction as a feature of contemporary parenting culture is certainly evident in Canada. "Shaming" occurs to such an extent that it too has become a subject for discussion in more mainstream media, both on- and offline.[74]

Who is doing the shaming? And who is likely to be judged? It seems that anyone online may be involved; this may explain the reluctance many parents now feel to engage in digital discussion. But they may also be vulnerable in the offline, real world, as that Winnipeg mother, introduced in the introduction, found to her cost, when city officials followed up a complaint that her children were unsupervised—in their fenced backyard. Critics comment that saturated media coverage of (rare but) negative news stories like Amber Alerts for missing children, the current intense focus on children's vulnerability, and an exaggerated view of what constitutes risk, all combine to make people more inclined to see danger where it doesn't exist. They make moral judgments—and the ubiquity of cell phones makes it easy for them to take action.

There is a certain inevitability to what often happens next. The story goes online, and others comment. People feel variously angry, or challenged, or sympathetic. If there is enough comment, mainstream media pick up the story as well. What may get reinforced in the process is the sense that strangers are not to be trusted—by parents, as well as by children . . .

Heightened consciousness of risk, and the desire to keep children as safe as possible, are cultural messages too. One of the best ways parents become aware of them is to compare their children's experiences with their own at the same age. Canadian clinical psychologist Alex Russell remembers the tree fort he and his cousins constructed over several summer holidays with extended family at their holiday cottage when he was a child. The fort was an amazing structure, high up in a tree, and made without any adult supervision. He remembers how much he enjoyed working on it, and how much he learned and grew from it. But he admits that he would never let his own children do anything similar. "The cultural shift towards protecting children has been strong enough to trump my own experience," he says.[75]

In conclusion . . .

I set out to discern the main messages that Canadian parents are likely to be hearing—a critical part of the "parenting culture" in which child-rearing here is done. What is probably clear from the foregoing is that my tuning in, highly selective though I knew it would be, picked up a complicated story.

In the Introduction I described the research, much of it from the UK, suggesting major changes over the previous decades in the way child-rearing was envisaged, with parents positioned as solely responsible for positive outcomes in their children, and the perception that they needed training for the *job* that parenting had become. That picture is a fair portrayal of "parenting" culture here too. The official messages combine to suggest that it is resolutely child-centred, with parents' responsibility for their children's cognitive, emotional, and physical development reinforced at many levels. The "support" offered, through various resources and programs, serves if nothing else to confirm official perceptions of its need. Those perceptions reinforce the view of parenting as a job, geared to outcomes for children, for which skills are needed that parents generally don't have. They are bombarded with opinion and advice, from both official and unofficial sources, on what they should be doing, and it tends to be mothers in particular who are most embroiled, and most stressed. Another element of stress is added with the shift in risk consciousness that positions children as innately vulnerable, and in need of constant protection and supervision.

Small wonder, then, that signs of resistance are also beginning to emerge. As one mother commented, in an online post to *Today's Parent*, "Every group I joined was part of an ongoing quest to learn tips and tricks that would help me survive motherhood, but I ended up feeling defeated by what I saw. I'm always seeking different perspectives and opinions, but instead I found hard lines drawn in the playground sand."[76] Her solution? To quit all Facebook parenting groups.

This is not to suggest that all online comment is negative. The gatherings of like-minded parents facilitated by social media may be immensely supportive, and may compensate for a shortage of actual, real-world help. Social media also allow for connections to distant family and friends—connections that my generation of parents had to forego. And this is to say nothing of the usefulness of search engines like Google for finding instant answers to practical questions. But one message is clear: there is a need to be selective.

There is also, now, an emerging message from many sources that parents need to be selective not just about parenting content on social media, but about parenting advice in general. Ironically, this too is "advice," and there are now books being written about it. One such book is by Canadian author Carl Honoré. It opens with the story of an art teacher describing his son as "gifted," Honoré's enthusiastic rush to find special art classes and programs, and his son having none of it. Honoré reports his son as saying, "I just want to draw. Why do grown-ups have to take over everything?"[77] The focus of the book is well summed up in its title: *Under Pressure: Rescuing Our Children from the Culture of Hyper-Parenting*.

Another book is by Alex Russell, cited earlier, who goes on from his treehouse recollections to question the cost of a parenting style that is so risk-averse and protective. He urges parents to "drop the worry ball" (the book's title), and instead try relinquishing some of the weighty responsibility they feel for every aspect of their children's lives.[78] In another book along these lines, Gordon Neufeld, cited earlier in the Gulli article, puts it even more strongly. He is scathing about the "multibillion-dollar industry of parental advice-giving" (though as noted earlier, he is a part of it). And he notes: "The reasoning behind parenting as a set of skills seemed logical enough, but in hindsight has been a dreadful mistake. It has led to an artificial reliance on experts, robbed parents of their natural confidence, and often leaves them feeling dumb and incompetent. . . . We miss the essential point that what matters is not the skill of the parents but the relationship of the child to the adult who is assuming responsibility."[79]

Today's parents, unlike those of my generation, are probably much more sceptical of the content of many of the messages they are getting about raising their children, because those messages are coming at them from so many different directions, and are so often contradictory. That scepticism may apply to the official advice too. As one of the readers of Gulli's article pointed out: "People are being told how to parent by a system that's not recognizing that every kid is different, as is every parent. There's no one right way for everyone."

Parents in Canada today may actually be better placed to take Spock's decades-old advice to "trust themselves." The messages are out there, delivered by both official and unofficial voices. Like many dominant messages, they tend to represent the voices of people accustomed to being heard, and perhaps speak most clearly to those able to choose how, and whether, to take them up. Not all parents are able, or willing, to do so. The factors that shape how parents might respond to the messages they hear is the focus of the next chapter.

2

Family portrait(s)

The last chapter explored the complicated network of messages that contribute to the culture of parenting in Canada—the informal rules and codes of conduct that parents are likely to be aware of, in the course of raising their children. What they make of this information is another question. No two families are exactly alike. Parents differ by the work they do, their age, their sexual orientation, their cultural heritage, whether or not they have partners, the number of kids they have—and those are just a few of the differences. The children in these diverse families are different too. All these differences shape how parents approach child-rearing, and what they are able to provide.

As I worked on this project, I talked to scores of parents, across the country, who reflected much of this diversity. The question underlying all our conversations was what raising children was like for them, in the context of all those expectations described earlier. Their experiences, and their reflections, appear in more detail in later chapters. But the final answer to that big question has to be: "it depends." Take the situation of Penny. When we spoke, she was living in a house in an attractive inner-city neighbourhood of Calgary, with her husband, 5-year-old son and, on a half-time basis, her 10-year-old stepson. She worked part-time as a geologist, in the company that had employed her full-time before her son's arrival. The part-time arrangement involved flexible hours to allow her to accommodate family responsibilities—for which she was mainly responsible, though she described her husband as "great with doing stuff with the kids." When her son was born, her widowed father and sister moved to Calgary to be near her and her family, and were "super, super involved." Her son, she said, "is all of ours."

Now take the situation of Richard. He was living in a small town in British Columbia when we met. He was soon to complete an undergraduate university degree. He was also about to become a father—for the fifth time. His complicated story began with an early and unhappy relationship which produced three children before their mother abandoned the family. It involved three years of sole custody and full-time caregiving to a trio of preschoolers, a return to university, a new relationship (with a single mother and fellow student), another baby, and the hope, finally, of a break from the short-term labouring or retail jobs of his past.

Or take Jessica, an immigrant from Korea, raising her 16-month-old daughter with her Canadian-born Chinese husband in another small British Columbia town. "For the parenting, there's a huge gap between Korea and here," she said. When we spoke she was spending some time nearly every day in a parent-and-tot group—and she was very much missing her mother. Or take Kyle, a self-employed graphic designer living in Vancouver with his wife and 2-year-old daughter. In our conversation he shared the family financial concerns—child-care too expensive to make it worthwhile for his wife to work, and housing costs needing to be factored in to the decision to have a second child. Or take Pamela, a single mother living in co-op housing and co-parenting her 10-year-old son with his remarried father . . .

These five parents exemplify some of the diversity noted earlier. They make it abundantly clear that the experience of raising children in Canada—and the extent to which the rules are followed—depend on a whole array of factors, some obvious and some not so obvious. In this chapter I set the experiences of these five, and some of the other parents I interviewed, in the broader context of family life in Canada. My focus here is necessarily on the big picture, on some of the factors that seem to be critical to any experience of raising children.

One clearly critical factor is how many parents are sharing the care on an ongoing basis. While families with two (usually married) parents continue to be the most common household arrangement, the proportion of one-parent families has increased—from 9 percent in 1976 to 20 percent of in 2014.[1] In 70 percent of single-parent families with children under 18 in 2011, the children lived with their mother; 15 percent lived with their father, and in 9 percent of cases children's time was divided equally between both parents' homes.[2] Single mothers are both more numerous than single fathers, and do more of the child-rearing work. Further complicating the issue of family work, of course, is the number of children requiring care. In 2016, 39 percent of couples with children had one child, and 42 percent had two. Only 18 percent had three or more.[3] Stepfamilies raising children from partners' previous unions are a growing phenomenon in Canada; a recent estimate suggests their numbers are comparable to the numbers of single parents.[4]

Another critical factor is parents' employment status. In Chapter 1 I noted the great increase over the past several decades in the proportion of dual-earner couples with dependent children, and the even more dramatic increase in the proportion of working mothers with children under 6 (from 32.1 percent in 1976 to 69.5 percent by 2015[5]). The *fact* of parents' employment, however, is only part of the story. From the perspective of their families, what *kind* of work they do matters too. A well-paying, secure job with predictable hours, benefits, some built-in flexibility, within reasonable commuting distance from home, would be any employed parent's ideal. And some parents, like one Ottawa mother I interviewed, have just that. Annette was a permanent professional employee in the federal civil service. She enjoyed benefits like topped-up maternity leave, the possibility of working a compressed work week, and an option to use income averaging for up to two five-week blocks of unpaid leave per year. She was thinking of using that time during the summer. Others are not so lucky. One single mother who participated in the project gave up a full-time job to start a house-cleaning business so she would have more flexibility to accommodate her school-age son's schedule. "[N]ow after five years, I'm at the point, just in the last six months . . . I'm wrestling with what I'm going to do next," she said. "Because I have no security . . . and my body is starting to feel the effects of the constant physical work, that's for sure."

Researchers examining paid employment in the current economic climate draw attention to the shift away from permanent, stable full-time jobs with benefits and opportunities for career growth, to jobs that are much less secure—or, in the language of this research field, more precarious. As one example, a major research study based at McMaster University, and examining employment in the Greater Toronto-Hamilton area, found that as many as 44 percent of workers have some level of precarity in their jobs.[6] The consequences for life at home when jobs are on contract, or pay no benefits, or involve unpredictable or on-call hours, or are not expected to last another year, hardly need to be spelled out.

Another dimension of work with clear family consequences is where people work in actual geographic terms. A major university research collaboration, appropriately called *On the Move*, is examining what it means, for individuals and families, when work is some distance away from home—involving either horrendously long commutes,[7] or (as is the case for many workers in the oil industry, for example), work shifts outside the home community that may last for weeks at a time.[8] The phenomenon of "working out West" or "working away" has long been a feature of working life in Newfoundland, for example.[9]

Even for people whose jobs have none of these disadvantages, work-family balance is often not easy, as researchers Linda Duxbury and Chris Higgins discovered. They have been studying just these issues among Canadian workers since 1991. Their third review, in 2011–2012, found that even in their predominantly well-educated professional sample of more than 25,000 full-time workers, many people struggled with workplace constraints. Most had fixed, 9-to-5 work hours; only a small proportion had flexibility in the form of a compressed work week (15 percent) or flex-time schedules (14 percent). Sixty percent worked more than 45 hours a week, and 54 percent took work home to complete outside regular working hours. There was little evidence of change in management support over the decades since the research began. Interviewed about the latest study at the time it was published, Duxbury commented: "Stress levels have gone up and life satisfaction has gone down . . . The bottom line is that many employees in our sample were having real difficulties balancing competing work and family demands."

Duxbury and Higgins also found that more women than men in the latest study had primary responsibility for child-care in their families, and were consequently more likely to experience stress.[10] The gender differences in the family division of earning and caring work noted by Duxbury and Higgins align with many other studies.[11] Mothers tend to do more of the household work, even when they are employed full-time—though as more recent research has discovered; this gender gap is very slowly closing.[12] In 2014 more than three-quarters of surveyed men in Canada reported engaging in unpaid household work (including child-care)—up from 51 percent in 1986.[13]

Mothers are also more likely to take parental leave on the birth or adoption of a baby—though here too parents' work situation and family income play a significant role in determining who will take leave, and for how long. Until early 2017, in all of Canada except Quebec, the federal Employment Insurance Act has offered a year of paid parental leave to eligible parents; fathers can share up to 35 weeks at 55 percent of average earnings up to a ceiling of $50,800. The province of Quebec opted out of the federal plan in 2006, and introduced its own Parental Insurance Plan. This plan offers less stringent eligibility requirements and more generous benefits than the federal plan, and includes three to five weeks of non-transferable paternity leave—the "daddy weeks" also available in some Scandinavian countries, notably Norway. (Not surprisingly, there has been a much greater uptake of leave by Quebec fathers—some 86 percent of eligible fathers had taken or intended to take leave in 2015, compared to 12 percent in the rest of Canada.[14]) The differences in take-up of paid leave among eligible mothers is also greater in Quebec—89.3 percent in 2013, compared to 64.3 percent in the rest of Canada.[15]

In its 2017 budget, the federal government announced an extension of parental leave from 12 months to 18 months, though benefits are not increased. While this extension is recognized as a potentially helpful option for some families, the proportion of parents able to take advantage of it is likely to be relatively small. Critics point out that the eligibility requirements for parental leave—in most cases 600 hours of insurable employment over the previous year—already eliminate many new parents.[16] Self-employed, part-time and casual contract employees would mostly fail to qualify. And then there is the financial penalty—perhaps not too serious in dual-earner families with sizeable professional earnings, but potentially deal-breaking in lower-income families, especially those living outside Quebec. (In 2013, 84 percent of Quebec mothers with household incomes under $30,000 received maternity and/or parental leave benefits, compared to only 43.6 percent in the rest of Canada.[17])

One official reason given for the extension of parental leave to 18 months is that child-care for infants younger than that is harder to find, and more expensive. But child-care for all preschool children in most of Canada is at a premium, and unaffordable for many parents. A recent extensive study estimated that there were regulated child-care centre spaces for only about 24 percent of Canadian children aged 0 to 5—a small proportion, given the numbers of children in this age group with two employed parents.[18] Availability and costs varied by province; in 2011 Quebec's subsidized universal program was most widely used, and was the least expensive at $152 per month (median) for children 4 and under. In Ontario, in contrast, the median was $652.[19] But costs are far higher in the major urban centres. A recent estimate put the median monthly cost of toddler-care at $1,375 in Toronto, and $1,325 in Vancouver. For preschoolers (aged 3 to 5) the median monthly cost was $1,150 in Toronto and $1,000 in Calgary.[20] New federal funding for child-care—aimed at making it more affordable and accessible to families in most need—was announced in June 2017. Child-care advocates however insist that quality child-care needs to be available to all Canadian children, and not just targeted populations.[21]

The shortage of regulated child-care places also accounts for the mix of child-care arrangements working parents make—and (depending on the age of the child) a great many parents need to make them. For example, in 2011 some 60 percent of parents of children aged 2 to 4 used outside child-care. For all children under 4, the mix included daycare (33 percent); home daycare, both licensed and unlicensed (31 percent); private arrangements, for example, relatives or nannies (28 percent); and preschool or nursery (9 percent).[22]

Child-care is probably one of the most stress-inducing elements of contemporary child-raising for working parents. And it is closely allied to another dimension of family life that poses huge challenges—the availability of support. It's worth revisiting that figure just quoted—the 28 percent of parents' child-care arrangements that involved "relatives or nannies." There's no breakdown within this group, but the chances are good that the "relatives" include grandparents who are providing child-care for a lucky minority of working parents. In the case of Christine, a very young mother coping with an unplanned baby in a rocky relationship and urgently wanting to return to work, a grandmother provided free full-time child-care for more than a year.

Demographic changes—in the form of population aging, declining fertility rates, and the postponing of parenthood—mean that there are actually more grandparents around now, and a proportionately smaller number of grandchildren. Across the country in 2011, some 8 percent of grandparents live with their grandchildren, mostly in three-generation households. The proportion is much greater though within certain groups—for example 11 percent among those claiming Aboriginal ancestry, and 22 percent in Inuit families. Among recent immigrants the proportion of co-resident grandparents is also high at 21 percent.[23] These figures speak to the significant role grandparents play in many Indigenous and immigrant families—a role that links to cultural values and practices as well.

Demographically, Indigenous families differ from the broader population in several ways. They have higher levels of common-law unions,

higher levels of mobility, and more children under 14 living at home. More
than a quarter of Indigenous children are living in households headed
by lone mothers.[24] Family life for many Indigenous families is shaped by
the trauma of the residential school experience, and its damaging consequences for the children and grandchildren of school survivors. Marlene
Brant Castellano, a member of the Mohawk Nation with extensive research experience on Indigenous issues, writes that in spite of the trauma,
"[t]he notion of the caring, effective, extended family, co-extensive with
community, continues to be a powerful ideal etched deep in the psyche
of [Indigenous] people."[25] Grandparents may be key players in attempts to
help families and communities aspiring to live up to this ideal.[26]

In 2016, more than one-fifth of Canadians were foreign-born. Some two
in five Canadian children under the age of 15 were either foreign-born, or
had at least one foreign-born parent.[27] For immigrant families, the challenge may be to balance the expectations of Canadian parents noted in the
previous chapter with those that may have dominated in their home countries. Sociologist Jeanna Parsons Leigh interviewed a father from Nigeria
in her study of immigrant families. He commented:

> I was told by [the instructor in a program he attended] that Canadi-
> an men share in the work of the home and the care of the kids. And
> this affirmed for me . . . what really I already knew, it was a demon-
> stration of how the Canadian family operates with busy schedules of
> both parents but also without much help or assistance from others.
> So, we learned that Canadians are very individual in their family
> relations. They don't have a lot of help per se. This is different than
> many other cultures like ours where help is readily there.[28]

His comment is particularly insightful. For many working parents, living (as most now do) at some distance from family, support like that received by Christine may not be available, from grandparents or any other
source. The now widespread use of social media to connect with family
and friends doesn't replace real-life, concrete help on the ground. For a
globalizing, mobile workforce, that kind of support may be in short supply.

Apart from the issue of geographic distance from other family members, where families live affects child-rearing in many other ways. Growing up on a farm, or in a small rural town where neighbours are well
known, will clearly be a different experience from growing up in a city. But
that rural experience is available to a diminishing minority of children—

more than 80 percent of Canadians live in urban areas.[29] And the urban experience is far from uniform. Exactly where families live, in those urban areas, also shapes the experiences of both parents and children. The suburban house with the fenced backyard may have been the ideal to which past generations of parents aspired. And in 2016, comprising 53.6 percent of dwellings, it was still the most common dwelling type. What's significant, though, are the differences in urban areas across the country. While cities like Calgary and Edmonton conform pretty closely to the Canadian average for detached homes, in the country's three biggest cities—Toronto, Montreal, and Vancouver—apartments are much more common.[30]

In Toronto, journalist Jackie Burns has written a children's book, an adventure story called *The Condo Kids*, to reflect the experience of her own children—and now, increasing numbers of other Canadian children—whose homes have balconies and elevators, and not backyards. In an article in the *Toronto Star*, Burns described the flourishing community of 50-some children in her building, where parents have come together to organize swimming lessons, a weekly chess club, floor hockey in the squash court, activities in the renovated games room, and outside play in the (communal) backyard. Burns commented: "All of this more than makes up for my kids not having their own backyard." [31]

In Vancouver in 2016, only 29 percent of homes were detached houses; 58 percent were apartments.[32] Vancouver researcher Nathan Lauster has noted that skyrocketing home prices in the city have made detached family homes unaffordable for many families; since 2006, more than half of Vancouver's children live in urban alternatives like apartments or row houses. He interviewed people to find out how housing mattered to their understanding of being parents. Some of his interviewees saw a house as a prerequisite to having children. Others, however, had moved beyond this view, and spoke positively of the benefits of alternative options. One of his interviewees, Katrina, a married mother who grew up in a house in a small town, now living in small apartment, commented:

A big suburban house, I think that's my biggest fear. A minivan household, you know? . . . I don't want to have the room where kids are separate from their families . . . and where, you know, people are watching TV in different locations. And where I have to drive my kids everywhere . . . where they can't do anything by themselves.[33]

In response to the rapidly growing proportion of families now living in high-rise apartments, the City of Toronto in early 2017 initiated a study called *Growing Up: Planning for Children in New Vertical Communities.*[34] This acknowledgement, both of children's needs and the changing environment in which they are growing up, represents a shift away from an earlier generation of urban planning organized, in the words of Montreal urban planner and academic Juan Torres, "for adults, and especially for adults with motor vehicles."

Suburbs of detached houses—the traditional ideal for family life, and the basis of urban planning around cars—look different from the way they looked in 1976, when only about one-third of couples with dependent children were dual-earners. What that meant, in the significant majority of families, was a parent (almost always the mother) at home during the day. As feminist scholars have pointed out, this was often far from ideal from the mothers' point of view. But their presence created a neighbourhood environment for children quite different from the silent daytime streets and empty parks of most Canadian residential areas today. In that era, too, most children walked or biked to a neighbourhood school. Today, as Torres notes, there is increasing centralization of schools, both to optimize resources and to offer specific programs, and children are either bussed there, or driven by parents. When parents have to drive their children everywhere, those children lose autonomy and independence. And Torres adds: "[W]hen parents drive children around, they aggravate the problems they are trying to avoid: an increase in traffic and accident risk, a decline in street conviviality, environmental degradation—things that make us perceive streets, neighbourhoods, and cities as unsuitable places for children."[35]

Urban sociologist Harry Hiller argues that parents are now creating communities in other ways. Instead of "communities of place," they create communities based on shared interests—often linked to their children's activities. Families may not know their neighbours, but may socialize instead around children's sports, or music, or other interests.[36] The difference, for children, is that parents are always present. In the words of Vancouver mother Katrina, quoted earlier, "they can't do anything by themselves."

The image of parents forging new groups around shared interests may also not conform to the lived reality of family life for many parents, who lack both the time and the money to participate. There's a connection here to many of the issues noted earlier: those sky-rocketing house prices, a more precarious labour market, and the shortage of affordable child-care in many Canadian cities. A research project called "Generation

Squeeze,"[37] based in Vancouver, draws attention to the multiple pressures on today's 30- and 40-year-olds, required to work harder and longer, often in less secure jobs, and with too few resources to support them as parents.

In conclusion . . .

All of the foregoing presents a rather sobering picture of the reality of child-rearing for many Canadian parents. Stressful and often also precarious work, a shortage of affordable child-care, distance from family and other means of practical or cultural support, neighbourhoods perceived as risky and unfriendly to children—all have consequences for family life, and for children's experiences growing up. Of course the story is not entirely negative. Parents in general are committed to their children, and they are resourceful. Some find ways around the challenges that are worth noting, and the chapters to follow contain many of these positive stories. To recall the discussion by author Jennifer Senior, introduced in the introduction, there is plenty of joy. But even for privileged parents, the fact remains that, on the basis of the issues discussed here, raising children in Canada today appears to be hard work.

Part II

Parents' Experiences

The four chapters to follow are based on my conversations with 84 parents, living in many different regions of Canada, who were willing to answer my big question: what raising children was like for them. Talking to parents was a way to give me some insight on Canada's "parenting culture" from the inside—from the people who were experiencing it directly.

They first learned about the project from the website I set up, called "The Parents and Children Project," which began to circulate in September 2016. The website contained some detail about what I was looking for, and information about my background as well. There was an email address that interested parents could use to contact me for more information.

I shared the website link with my own circle of friends, former students and colleagues, and with other contacts I thought would be interested in the project. From there it travelled across the country, and on to the various devices of parents in many different circumstances. In these days of Facebook and other social media, it's of course impossible to say where it actually went. Friends passed it on to friends, but they also passed it on to other people they knew would be interested, and in some cases to parent-related groups they themselves were involved in. The project description seemed to strike a chord.

Many of the early responders were the people who are often the most keen to assist with research on family-related topics: mothers, mostly well educated and professionally trained if not currently employed. They provided invaluable contributions, but they were only part of the story. I needed to reach out in a few specific directions, to involve those whose voices I hadn't heard enough of—fathers, and, more generally, people from more diverse cultural and income backgrounds. That was more challenging, but thanks to the help of several community organizations and parent networks I approached directly,[1] I was able to touch some of those demographic bases as well.

In the end, I was able to include 49 mothers and 35 fathers. Mothers ranged in age from 27 to 48, and fathers from 30 to 50. But about half of all the parents were in their 30s, raising preschoolers. Though not all were professionally employed, they were a well-educated group—almost all had some level of post-secondary education.[2]

There were residents of every province of the country except Newfoundland and Labrador. (In spite of my best efforts, I could not persuade any Newfoundland parents to participate.) But participants tended to cluster in several key urban areas; about a quarter lived in Calgary, and a similar proportion in major urban centres in Ontario. This was in fact a predominantly urban group. It was also predominantly white. I noted earlier my attempts to connect with people from more diverse backgrounds, and I found just a few who were willing to speak with me. They represent a tiny proportion of the group, but I have tried to ensure that their voices are included.

Conventionally, researchers talk about interviews and interviewing, but I felt that my conversations with parents were just that—conversations. I had an agenda, with certain questions about their backgrounds and experiences that I wanted to make sure were addressed. But parents themselves raised issues I hadn't thought of, and we covered a lot of new ground. I wanted them to tell me what raising kids in Canada today was like for them, and that's just what they did. I met in person with about a quarter of the parents (all those in Calgary, but also some in other Alberta centres, and in Vancouver and Toronto.) In other cases we talked by phone, or over skype. All the parents gave me permission to record our conversations.

I talked with parents between September 2016 and March 2017. In the months that followed, I listened again to the audio files, took notes, and thought carefully about how to set up what I had heard. Parents were reporting from different stages on the journey: some were adjusting to their first baby, others were coping with toddlers and older preschoolers, and still others had children nearly ready for high school. And though those stages were being experienced by different parents, and different children, I thought the stages would be a useful organizing device, since the early years always play forward and shape what happens later on.

In Chapter 3, I introduce nine parents who were caring for babies in their first year of life—the year that marks the start of the parenthood journey, and one that merits particular attention because of how life-changing it is. Chapter 4 introduces the larger group of 43 parents whose caregiving was mostly centred on toddlers and preschoolers. This chapter looks at how families grow, from the first baby to (usually, but not invariably) a sibling or two. It also considers how parents divide up the work of caregiving, and how those divisions, too, can play forward. Chapter 5 looks more closely at the *detail* of child-rearing in the preschool years. Finally, Chapter 6 introduces the 32 parents who were raising older children. It too looks at the ways mothers and fathers are sharing the caregiving work, and explores the issues they confront as parents with children well established in school. In every case, parents' names and occasionally other potentially identifying details have been changed to ensure confidentiality.

I have noted already that this group of parents, though coming from a diverse set of backgrounds that I try to acknowledge, is by no means statistically representative of parents across the country. It is not representative in another important way. The fathers who responded to my appeal for participants were, as far as I could tell from our conversations, highly engaged in the work of child-rearing—far more engaged than is the case (as noted in Chapter 2) for Canadian fathers in general. This outcome is hardly surprising; disengaged fathers would be unlikely to want to share their experiences. But as Chapter 2 also notes, times are changing, and fathers are changing too. The fathers I introduce here are collectively signs of that change.

3

Becoming parents

For all parents, the arrival of the first baby is a life-changing event. Even for parents who have had some prior contact with young children, there is nothing in their lives to which it can be compared, and no way to know what the experience of raising this particular child will be like. Babies are delivered to families in widely different circumstances, as the previous chapter indicated. Those circumstances can be critical in shaping the experience of parenthood, and they can start exerting an influence right from a baby's birth.

Parents of new babies are at the start of a journey. This journey will unfold on a path, a trajectory, that will only become visible retrospectively, when enough time has passed to allow for some looking back. Trajectories are never pre-determined, and they are always open to change. But they always have a beginning in the early months. What happens then can cast a long shadow—so beginnings are worth a close look.

In this chapter I share the beginning stories of nine parents, whose experiences illuminate some of the diversity of family circumstances, and the culture of parenting that surrounds them, as they make it through the first year.

The early months

Of all the contributors to this research project, 37-year-old Patricia was the newest parent. She was the mother of 11-week-old Rosie, whose visiting grandmother brought her to be nursed while Patricia and I had tea in the kitchen of their Toronto home.

The breastfeeding was going well, and the grandmother (Patricia's mother), who had been visiting from her home outside Toronto for much of Rosie's young life, had been in Patricia's judgment an essential support.

"From Day 1 she was here," Patricia said. "Thank God! I was totally clueless." Not only was this grandmother an invaluable source of information about how to handle the baby, but she had also been on hand to do a lot of the caregiving herself.

This was also much needed. Patricia was a business consultant, currently self-employed and working from home on some major contracts. Though there was a lot of flexibility in these arrangements, the work was demanding—and so was the baby. She arrived when Patricia was in the middle of a project, and in those first few days nobody was getting any sleep.

The sleep issue looms very large for most parents of newborns. Patricia reported that she and her husband had "read all the literature, [watched] all the YouTube videos." They were well aware of what they were supposed to do, which was to have the baby sleep in a bassinet by their bed. But "she didn't like that." So they tried (on the advice of another parent), a much more expensive piece of equipment—a bassinet that could swivel over the parents' bed, to keep the baby close, but still safely separate. (It could also vibrate, and play lullabies at the push of a button.) But baby Rosie didn't like that either. She just wanted to be held. "I saw the sun go down, and come up, and I thought, I can't sustain that," she recalled. Eventually, things got better—but only because she took the baby into bed with her. "I wake up with her in all weird positions . . . but it's the only way we've been able to sleep," she said. "We're basically breaking all the rules."

Patricia's Chinese mother would not agree that rules were being broken. "My mom slept with me in the bed, and my grandmother with my mother," Patricia said.

> But now I guess, talking about parenting, there's so much information, like access to information is so diverse. So you have all these different opinions . . . When I was pregnant, a lot of people had advice. I didn't realize that after you have the baby, then you *really* hear, oh, you should do that, and don't ever do this. And so I had all these ideas of what we should be doing. But the thing that actually worked was, you know, against all of that . . . We are attachment parenting not by choice!

Patricia said she had no time for the online debates. But she had been going to a baby circle for mothers and babies, run by the community nurse at the local community centre. There she discovered that "everyone in the room" was co-sleeping. "It was very comforting to know that we weren't unusual, or the only ones," she said. The baby circle gave her the opportunity to meet other babies, and compare them to Rosie. She had concluded that Rosie was not like them. "She's very headstrong, and if she's not happy she'll let you know it," she said. "She came out of the womb like that, very headstrong and loud. It's totally been life-changing."

The baby circle also allowed her to meet other mothers, most of whom were not doing outside work. "A lot of the moms hang out afterwards, but I'm rushing off because I've got a meeting," she said. "I've got to work!" It was only at the last circle she attended that she met another working mother—also self-employed, with a 6-month-old baby:

It was like looking in a mirror. That was really interesting for me. Her mind was somewhere else . . . It was good for me to see that other mothers were at work, and still having that career in addition to being a new mom. But it was also scary, because I realized, she couldn't relax, she was very, I would say, stressed out, and tense.

Patricia was aware that her commitment to her own work was making her life as a new mother very much more complicated and demanding. But it was also, as she put it, her "lifesaver":

I still have a connection to my identity outside of just being a mom, and I still feel like I am able to have a life [that] I didn't have to sacrifice, just because I have a baby . . . And I did notice, when I was in the circle, sharing with other moms, they really do feel like, I don't talk to any adults, I need to get out of the house, I have no outlet. I see myself, I could definitely be that person. But I'm forced to, because of the work I'm doing, to talk to other adults, and I'm forced to throw on some clothes and go see the world. But I have to organize, tremendously, just to get that. For every hour I'm away, it's like, a big deal.

Patricia was aware that, happy as she was about being self-employed, she was going to need to make some changes. Her days—and nights—involved multi-tasking, often with a nursing baby on one arm, and her phone handy for messages in the other hand. "I just can't do the hours I've been doing, and I cannot [bend] to provide the kind of service I had been providing," she said. "And it's just me. It's not like I have a whole team."

Lacking a team for her work, she knew she would need a team at home to "support the machine." Around Rosie's birth she had hired a doula.

Later she hired a nanny, who turned out not to be suitable. When we talked, the question of child-care was pressing, but also unresolved. In the short term, her mother was saving the day.

What her mother was also doing was not so much *dis*placing as *re*placing a husband who was not as engaged as Patricia thought he would be. He too worked from home, and seemed to think that his mere presence in the house, and his support with cooking and cleaning, constituted involvement. There had been very little hands-on help. "He's changed two diapers, maybe three," she said. His detachment was a source of some distress; there had been many fights about it. But she was aware of his total unfamiliarity with babies and their needs, and noted that now, as Rosie was becoming more sociable, her father would carry her more. He had yet to be left to care for the baby on his own. At the same time, he had strong views on how the baby should be handled, which tended not to coincide with those of Patricia's mother. Sleep training was under discussion. Meanwhile Patricia was trying to accommodate everyone. "I am struggling with, what's the best for my baby, my relationship with my husband, I really need the support from my mom . . ." she said.

Patricia's experience, after only 11 weeks, draws attention to many of the factors, noted in the last chapter, that shape the experience of parenthood over the long term: whether the caring work is shared with a partner; whether there is other support (especially practical, hands-on help); whether there are resources available to hire or buy what's needed to make the job easier; whether (and how) paid work is balanced with child-care; whether outside messages about the "right" thing to do are taken on board, or modified, or ignored—and whether those messages are filtered through different cultural understandings. That's to say nothing of the personal(ity) differences between babies, and between parents—differences that can sometimes overwhelm all the others. These factors also played in to the experiences of the eight other new parents who shared their stories with me.

Anne, a 34-year-old mother in Ottawa, was nearly as new to parenting as Patricia. Her son Matthew was four months old, and in those four months Anne's life, like Patricia's, changed in ways that she had never anticipated. "I had so many thoughts about how things were going to go, and they one hundred percent did not go in that direction," she said. It had been a very difficult transition, starting with Matthew's premature birth. Soon there were worries about his weight and the need for formula supplements, and then there were difficulties with breastfeeding. By the time Anne and I talked, breastfeeding had been almost completely abandoned. The "life lesson" she was learning was that, when it came to the baby, she wasn't in control.

Anne was a highly educated professional, like Patricia deeply committed to her work. She was on parental leave that was being tapered to an end so that she could take up a new and demanding job. Like Patricia, Anne was facing the challenge of combining motherhood with work that was extremely important to her. She commented:

> How do I balance who I am, the things I have been using as a marker of my identity for a really long time, and that sense of wanting to spend a lot of time with Matthew, but also finding it a bit overwhelming? . . . Becoming a mom is really weird and it's unsettling . . . I don't know how to do this, and I don't know if I *can* do this . . . I do want to enjoy him. It's just, how do you package all that together?

Enjoyment had been hard to find. Matthew didn't sleep well, and needed to be held all the time. Anne said that she "wore" the baby (in a sling) all day long. Matthew usually started off the night in his bassinet, but if he was restless Anne would take him into bed with her. He slept the first two months or so of his life on his mother's chest. Anne said, "I know SIDS is there, but . . ." The risk, she felt, needed to be put into context. Like Patricia, she was doing what seemed to work.

She "wore" the baby because it seemed to be what the baby wanted—and she remembered as an undergraduate student reading an anthropological study of mothering round the world, which demonstrated that wearing babies and co-sleeping were global phenomena. Though many other mothers have used findings like these as evidence in support of attachment parenting—which they might also claim characterized Anne's approach—that was not the label Anne applied. In fact she was averse to labels, and to parenting books in general. "We're going to do things a bit more organically," she said.

Both Anne and Patricia were struggling to find their way in the new and unfamiliar world of baby care, while retaining their commitment to careers that were either ongoing or about to resume. But there were also significant differences in their situations. Where Patricia's partner was disengaged, Anne's husband Colin could hardly have been more involved. He had been hands-on from the start, getting up in the night with her every time the baby needed attention, and more recently taking on much of that night time care once they switched to formula feeding. I talked to Colin too, and our conversation resonated with his attachment to Matthew and his commitment to fully sharing his care.

Colin also talked about the early difficulties—the premature birth, the problems with breastfeeding, and the (necessary) early focus on Anne and Matthew. At first, he could only be an observer. "I definitely had times when I just wasn't feeling that connection," he said. "It was just another chore I had to do, rather than another person I was connecting with." But the night time care changed things. "I'm a much better person in terms of the night-time activities anyway," he said. "Anne has a much harder time getting up." Being able to feed Matthew made a big difference. "When you're feeding him, and he looks at you and smiles, it doesn't matter that you're exhausted, you're helpless to it . . . I've been enjoying that aspect of it, for sure . . ."

Even with his support, caring for Matthew had been a struggle. When, a few weeks before our conversation, he had fallen ill with an infection, they had called on Anne's parents for help. These were grandparents willing and able to drop everything and respond in a crisis—but they lived 12 hours away. There was no-one closer whom Anne and Colin thought they could call on. Anne had an online network she described as "phenomenal" in its support, but asking for practical help from friends closer at hand was something both she and Colin balked at. "We're all just too polite," Anne said.

Instead, lacking the full-time care of a resident grandmother that Patricia and her husband could count on, they had hired the help they needed. It took the form of child-care for Matthew two days a week in a day home. They envisaged that some form of that arrangement would continue, with Anne able to organize her work to have every Friday off, and Colin, a computer programmer, able to work at least some of the time from home. Colin was committed to doing at least his 50 percent share of the caregiving, and perhaps becoming the primary caregiver if Anne's career developed as they hoped it would.

In the midst of the struggles, he had clear ideas about what he wanted for Matthew as he grew up—an environment where he would be free to explore, and make mistakes, where he would not be afraid to ask questions, where he could play without the expectation of specific developmental outcomes. His philosophy was in large part a reflection of his own experience as a child, growing up in a country setting where "you pretty much did what you wanted." He was aware that Matthew would probably not have that freedom:

> I know it will be a little bit more difficult because of—political correctness isn't the right term for it, but there's very much an "everybody's watching" type aspect . . . You have to appease the social influences that are in your living environment, otherwise your living environment will become very difficult.

He was already discovering the change that Matthew's presence was making to his own experience of his living environment:

> People just did not talk to me before we had Matthew. When I was out and about, it would rarely happen that I would have a conversation with a stranger. I would almost say never . . . And now if I'm out with Matthew by myself it's almost a guarantee that I'm going to be in a conversation with somebody, [about] how things are going, their kids as well . . .It seems like once you have a young baby like this, you're part of a public conversation that you were not included in before.

Colin liked, and was intrigued by, this change—and it *was* a change, for a man who acknowledged that previously he had barely spoken to any of his neighbours. But he also recognized, as Anne did too, that his benign reception probably had something to do with the fact that he was a father. Mothers faced a higher bar, and encountered more disapproval. Anne had felt it because Matthew was already in child-care. The fact that he was likely to be an only child also drew comments. (Anne's response to those comments was to suggest that parents making them must have had a very different early experience—or were just not as worried about things as she was.) Anne shared Colin's views about giving Matthew freedom to explore. She didn't want to be a "helicopter parent"; it would be important for Matthew to develop coping skills on his own. She would try not to hover when it came time for play in the park—but also knew that it would be hard to do. "If I go to the park, and check my emails, people are going to be judging me," she said.

But playing in the park was still a long way off, for Rosie in Toronto and Matthew in Ottawa. Their parents, still in the first months of parenthood, were in survival mode. They were stressed and sleep-deprived, still learning how to respond to their babies' needs, and not at all sure if, or when, life would get easier.

Getting past survival mode

Many parents could tell them that the 6-month mark is often the turning point. Babies' sleep patterns become (usually, though not invariably) a little more predictable. Often they are starting to eat some solid food—a shift that may reduce demands on breastfeeding mothers in particular. They are also much more sociable, responding to attention with smiles and coos. They are starting to turn from babies into little people.

Evan, also in Ottawa, was enjoying just this shift with 7-month-old Jason, and was at home full-time to experience it. Like Colin, Evan was a deeply involved father. He was in fact taking on the lion's share of parental leave, and had been Jason's full-time caregiver since his wife Melissa returned to work three months earlier. Sharing the leave in this way was a strategic decision. Melissa, a federal public servant, was new in her job, and was needed for a project whose completion she had to oversee. Evan, with more seniority in his job, was better placed to take the extra time, even though doing so was a big step. His workplace was technically supportive, but culturally somewhat masculinist in its expectations of men as workers and fathers. It was not the fact of the leave, but its length, that might raise eyebrows.

But Evan wanted to take the time anyway, partly to give himself the chance to explore other employment options. And so far, after a few bumpy patches, the leave was going well. At first, Melissa would come home at lunchtime to breastfeed the baby. (Evan commented: "The social pressure to breastfeed is incredible!") But that soon changed; Jason, spending much more time with his father, was happy to be bottle-fed, so Melissa switched to pumping breast milk instead.

Another challenge came with Jason's dependence on Evan's (and only Evan's) rocking to get him to sleep. "I tried to go to a hockey game once, and I had to leave in the third period," he recalled. "He woke up and wouldn't go back to sleep." Aware that they needed a new strategy, on the recommendation of a friend they hired a sleep consultant to give them advice. She assessed where Jason was sleeping, and his sleep patterns, made some recommendations, and followed up with phone and email support. It was, Evan thought, the kind of help that might be given by "a grandma or a great-grandma . . . if you don't have access to one." In the absence of an actual grandma—both Evan's and Melissa's families lived far away—the sleep consultant's advice did help. Jason was sleeping better by the time Evan and I talked.

"I don't have a huge amount of reference, but I think he's pretty easy-going," he said: "He's always been pretty good. He's pretty chill during the day, and he loves to hang out. I believe we have it pretty easy." In that sense, he and Melissa were in a better position than Anne and Colin, who were still in survival mode, and struggling. But both couples were similarly placed in terms of close-at-hand support. There wasn't much they could call on. Melissa, back at work, was in touch again with her work friends. Evan, still doing some work from home, was in touch with his too. But like Colin he didn't have anyone at work he was close to—or at any rate close enough to talk with about babies. He and Melissa were far from their own parents and good friends; for now, the virtual community was more important than the one they actually lived in.

In fact, he worried about the possibility of Jason growing up in a city like Ottawa, and never having the kind of connection to nature he had as a child growing up on the west coast. He wondered about having a cottage, where Jason could roam, and be in the woods. "I worry about that a lot, even though it seems like a long way away," he said. "I worry about that a fair amount. I don't really think it's the same here."

But like Colin, Evan was beginning to see his physical community in a new way. He had noticed that the park nearby seemed to be used by a collective of parents. "I don't remember this from when I was growing up, but there's always all these random toys around the park, and people leave them there," he said. "It's really cool actually—I like it."

Visits to the park were still some time away for Jason, too. The more immediate issue would be Evan's return to work, and Jason's transfer to an institutional day-care centre near their home. Evan had mixed feelings about this change. If there were compelling reasons for going back to work before the year of parental leave was over, he would consider them. But an early return seemed unlikely. "As he gets older, and more interesting and more interactive, I think that's just going to lessen any desire to go back to work," he said. "He's so wonderful, and very precious. I'm so grateful to have him in my life. I didn't know how great he would be."

Evan most clearly articulated the joy that was building from his experience of caring for Jason. Joy was also at the forefront of my interview with the parents of 9-month old Chloe, in Edmonton. Chloe was adopted at birth, so there was no pregnancy recovery needed, and no struggles with breastfeeding, since it wasn't an option. But to those practical realities could be added the fact that Chloe slept through the night almost from birth—at first in a tray on their bed, then in a bassinet beside the bed, then (at about 6 months) in her own room.

Chloe's parents had more reason for joy than the fact that she was an easy baby. As gay men, both had gone through a period of thinking they would never be parents at all, though it was something Owen said he had wanted all his life. They had several nieces and nephews, and thought they could be the "cool gay uncles" instead. "Owen was more inclined than I was, though I hadn't ruled it out," Nathan said. What changed, for Nathan, was the birth of a baby to some good friends. "It was the first time I had ever really spent time with a newborn," he said. He described himself as a "very analytical" kind of person, who couldn't until then come up with a good reason for having children. He learned from that newborn that the decision to have a baby wasn't amenable to rational calculus; sometimes you just knew it was what you wanted.

Once Nathan was committed, the adoption process unfolded smoothly and rapidly. "We had a stellar experience," Nathan said. "It turns out gay men have an advantage in adoption!" (There is some evidence that they may be favoured in open adoptions by birth mothers who know there will be no other mother to replace them.) They were present for the delivery; Nathan cut the cord, and Owen had the first skin-to-skin contact with Chloe.

From this happy beginning, it seemed that there had been no going back. There was strong support from family and friends—Owen commented that some people actually cried with happiness for them, on hearing that the adoption had been approved. After nine months, the support had not wavered. With Chloe's arrival, Owen had taken three months' leave from his business manager job. When we spoke, they were handling Chloe's care in shifts. Nathan, an IT consultant who worked from home, was in charge during the day. Owen was able to work a compressed work week, so was home every other Friday. He also took over on evenings and weekends. Nathan's parents took care of Chloe one afternoon a week, and another friend who wanted to spend time with Chloe came in one afternoon a week also. Information and advice also came less from online sources than from people they knew—friends who included a nurse/paramedic and a doctor, and Owen's sister, who had had a baby a year or so before Chloe's arrival.

They lived in a progressive urban neighbourhood, and their friends were close by. And as well-educated professional white men, they were confident that they could handle any criticism of their less conventional family, should it arise. But they didn't think it would. Owen commented: "I kind of had this realization that us having a child brings us closer to the norm for families."

First birthdays

A baby's first birthday is a significant milestone. In most cases the worst (in terms of sleep deprivation and feeding problems) is over. The baby, though still a baby, is no longer quite so fragile and vulnerable. And a year's worth of intimate connection gives parents a stronger sense of who the baby is; they now have some history to work with. As babies become toddlers, it's time to think about what comes next. In many working families, there are practical decisions to be made; the one-year mark may be a time of transition in child-care, as parental leave ends and other arrangements need to be made. But however children are to be cared for, there is usually a shift in focus for parents—new worries about risk and safety as babies become mobile, and often a consciousness of other responsibilities associated with new stages of development.

Kathy, Larry, and Andrea, the three parents I talked to whose babies had just reached the one-year milestone, presented a thought-provoking mix of similarities and contrasts with the parents introduced earlier in the chapter. There were hints from all three of particular trajectories of caring starting to be established.

In Kathy's family, and in Larry's, deeply involved fathers supporting mothers' professional careers—familiar from the stories of Anne and Colin, and Evan—were at the one-year mark taking over or continuing as primary at-home caregivers. In both cases, with a few rough patches, the caregiving was going smoothly, with one-year-olds who were sleeping better, and parents who were indeed able to plan for what might be needed next. They too were thinking about cognitive development, and the value of free play, and how they would handle the judgments of others (in both cases, confidently). And they too could call on family members (in Kathy's case a sister, in Larry's a mother-in-law) to provide back-up. Like all the parents introduced so far, they were relatively privileged, experiencing stress and making decisions in a context in which options were available and choices were possible. Andrea's story was a sobering counterpoint.

I first met Andrea at a focus group in a non-profit agency offering support to Indigenous families. In a phone conversation later she told me more about her background, and how the first year of her son Peter's life had gone. In a word, it had been difficult.

Andrea had spent the year at home, and was managing almost entirely alone. This was not because her partner was unwilling to help, but rather because he needed to work seven days a week to support the family. Andrea would have liked to work too, but said that the cost of child-care ruled out that possibility.

There had been problems with the baby from the start, with birth complications that kept him in hospital for five days. Then came problems with breastfeeding. Andrea had wanted to breastfeed exclusively, and the baby took to nursing right away. But he wasn't gaining weight. "They said he wasn't getting enough nutrients from it," she said. Her pediatrician recommended a switch to formula, and though other people told her she could continue to nurse as well, she followed the pediatrician's advice, and gave up nursing. The switch had financial, as well as emotional consequences; this was a cash-strapped family, and formula feeding cost money where breastfeeding did not.

Andrea said that Peter had not been diagnosed as a colicky baby, but for the first three months he cried as much as one. At three months, briefly, he started to sleep through the night. "But now he's gone backwards again!" she said. He was waking through the night again, and needing to be fed. He wasn't falling properly asleep till about 4 a.m. All the advice she was hearing was that she should let him cry, but that was difficult, because the crying wouldn't stop. And he did seem to be a baby who needed to be fed; at a year old, he was on the 35th percentile for weight, and the 85th for height. Andrea said that when he was about 8 months old, those who had been concerned about his weight earlier were starting to say, "Well, that's probably what his physique is going to be—tall and lean." Andrea, thinking of tall lean men on both sides of the family, said her response was, "I told you that at three months old."

Peter was born to a mother who, at 33, had far more experience of child-care than all of the other mothers introduced so far. Andrea had helped her own mother run a day home, had cared for her little sister "most of the time," and had worked as a nanny. But even that experience didn't diminish the challenges posed by her own baby. And there was no outside support. They lived in an apartment building, where the neighbours kept to themselves. Sometimes, she visited her mother—an hour-and-a-half bus ride, since she didn't drive. That would give her an hour to hang out, but her mother was busy too, and not able to take over. Other family members, though not out of the province, were also too far away to help.

It might have been that family support would not have been her first choice in any case. She noted that she "didn't have a great experience" growing up. But that made her determined to raise her own child positively, finding "light and sunshine" instead of being negative and getting angry. She did not want to talk about her Indigenous background, beyond noting that it was "in the blood line." But it was the Indigenous family agency that was, as she put it, "keeping me sane."

She found it through a contact in a Facebook group. (For Andrea too, digital connections compensated for the absence of other kinds. In her case, the connections were Facebook buy-and-sell groups, through which mothers traded diapers, formula, and baby clothes.) The contact introduced her to a post-natal group at the agency, and she later joined one of its other moms' groups. This one had turned into a support group. "It's amazing, so I have to do it," she said. It brought otherwise isolated mothers together to talk. There was also an agency organizer who could be consulted, and occasionally professionals were brought in to speak about a range of issues. Andrea got connected to a 6-week nutritional program that also offered the practical help of a monthly bag of vegetables, from which she could make her own baby food.

Slowly, these mothers' group connections were starting to strengthen. There was some late night texting—because, Andrea joked, her moms' group friends knew that, if they were up with a baby at 3 a.m., Andrea was likely to be up too. One of the group mothers took up her invitation to come to Peter's first birthday, a week before we talked, and "really enjoyed herself." Andrea hoped there would be more shared birthday celebrations.

But even in the moms' groups, there was no real respite. The baby was always there—he was present in his carrier during our focus group meeting (and sleeping, which was a surprise to the moms who knew him). In fact he was almost never out of Andrea's sight. Her husband helped as much as he could when he was home, but his relentless work hours meant he was as tired as Andrea, and she was reluctant to hand over the baby for that reason. "It's hard on the two of us," she said. Sometimes, she was on a short fuse.

My talk with Andrea did not cover issues like Peter's future cognitive development or her ideas about free play. Andrea was thoughtful and articulate, with considerable child-care experience. Under other circumstances she would probably have had a lot to say about those issues. But not now. Thinking about cognitive development and free play must take place in a context in which more fundamental needs are being met. That was not the case for Andrea. "The stressful thing is, it comes down to finances," she said. Lacking money, she was resourceful enough to take advantage of help where it was available. Her involvement with the agency and all it could offer would, in the short term, have to be enough.

In conclusion . . .

It's clear, from all these stories, that many factors combine to shape the experience of early parenthood. Those suggested earlier—partner involvement, work situations, external support, financial resources, among others—could be seen to make a difference, sometimes easing the path, and sometimes making it more difficult. There were differences too in the extent to which the dominant messages of this stage, notably relating to feeding and sleep, were taken up. (On the whole, they were heard, especially by mothers, but not necessarily heeded.) There were differences too in the style of individual parents, and in the demands of individual babies. (It's hard not to wonder how the early months would have gone for Anne and Colin, or for Andrea, if their babies had been as easy to care for as Chloe.)

The first year is just the start of the journey. Next steps take parents in many different directions, as the chapters to follow will show.

4

Families with preschoolers

In the last chapter, I introduced parents in the first year of their first baby's life, and suggested some of the factors that, even at that early stage, were starting to make a difference to their caregiving experience. Beyond that first year, there are of course many changes, starting with the babies themselves. They become toddlers, and start to explore the world. At about age 3, they have developed physically, socially, and cognitively to the point where they start to be thought of as preschoolers. And at 5, in most provinces, they're getting ready to take the big step towards school.[1] The experiences of these early years, for both parents and children, are also significantly shaped by the arrival—or the non-arrival—of a sibling or two.

In this chapter I introduce parents who had made it through the first year, and were at various stages along the road of toddler and preschooler caregiving. Most, like Patricia, introduced in the previous chapter, had had no prior experience of children in their lives before becoming parents. (One father, recalling the trip home from hospital with the first baby, commented, "I can't believe they let us out of there.") But by the time we spoke, they had learned a great deal.

Nineteen of them (nine mothers[2] and 10 fathers) were caring for single children, whose ages ranged from 16 months to nearly 5. Six of them were expecting a second baby.[3] Seventeen parents (11 mothers[4] and six fathers) already had two children under 6. Two more (one mother and one father) each had three under 6. Five parents (four mothers and one father) were still immersed in preschool caregiving, but also had older children who had just started school.

These basic number counts tell only part of the story. Behind them is a history of family planning (or absence of planning), and the parental joy or grief or anxiety or relief that is another part of the story, as families form and change. The arrival, or non-arrival, of siblings has consequences for all concerned—consequences that last a lifetime, and that start taking effect early. So in this chapter I look more closely at the family configurations the number counts represent. I then move to a more detailed examination of the way caregiving is set up in these households during the busy preschool years.

Configurations of family

Most parents, however many children they end up having, spend at least some time in a one-child family. After the first baby arrives, the question they confront—and the question others inevitably ask them—concerns a second baby. The assumption on the part of others is usually that there *will* be a second, and the question slides to *when*, rather than *if*. Of the one-child parents I talked with, *when* and *if* turned out to be important differentiators.

One—and only one

For the parents of the youngest babies, it was sometimes just too soon to be thinking about adding a second. (Larry, the father of the one-year-old introduced in the last chapter, joked that his answer when family members asked about a second baby was that he'd like to get eight hours' sleep a night before deciding.) Some parents knew they wanted a second baby, but were biding their time. But other parents I talked with were more committed to having only one child. They tended to fit into one of four scenarios.

The first was linked to parents' age, and ideas about family size. Babies born to older mothers with professional jobs to which they were committed were likely to be only babies. In some cases, like Karen's, the decision to have a baby followed a long and successful career, and the often-cited biological clock starting to tick in her 30s. Karen said she and her husband decided, "We can do this now! . . . And we knew it was just one." Their baby was born when Karen was 36. In Marie's case, there was some negotiation involved. She wanted children, but her husband, who had a child in a much earlier relationship, would only consider one. Eliot and his wife had been trying to conceive for many years before their "miracle baby" was born. Eliot was 50 when we spoke; another baby seemed unlikely.

The second was directly linked to finances. In Chapter 2 I introduced

Kyle, a self-employed graphic designer living in Vancouver with his wife and 2-year-old daughter. I noted then the dilemma that Kyle and his wife were confronting—child-care too expensive to make it worthwhile for his wife to work, a second baby probably requiring a housing move, and housing costs in the city too high to be affordable on one income.

The third scenario included parents whose first babies had not been planned, and whose circumstances virtually guaranteed there would not be a second. These babies were even more life-changing than babies usually are, but their parents were no less devoted. Diane got pregnant in the course of a short relationship which would probably have ended otherwise. But from the beginning, the father was as committed as she was to keeping, and caring for, the baby. When she discovered the pregnancy, they reconnected briefly, then separated when their son Paul was 7 months old. When Diane and I spoke, Paul was 3, and both parents were continuing an unconventional but equitable sharing of his care. Clive's son was also the product of a short-term relationship. In this case though, Clive found out about the pregnancy only when the baby's mother was in the process of arranging to have him adopted. Clive, at 47, surprised himself and everyone who knew him by deciding that he wanted to raise the baby himself. When we spoke, the baby was 20 months old, and Clive was his full-time, and sole, caregiver.

The fourth scenario was poignantly illustrated by two mothers for whom the experience of delivering and caring for the first baby was so distressing and difficult that having a second seemed unthinkable. Gina's story was particularly painful. She had grown up thinking she would be a stay-at-home mother to many children. For several years, she had been in a relationship with a man who was much less sure about having children, and they broke up for a while for that reason. When they got back together, she got pregnant almost immediately, and not intentionally. For many reasons, it was a difficult time. "Once I was pregnant, I expected to be more excited than I was," she said.

> But I think, because I had just taken some time, and had started figuring out who I was and how I wanted to live my life, and now all of a sudden all of that got put on hold . . . I wasn't as excited as I thought I would be.

What started out as perhaps just a problem of timing was soon compounded by other crises. Her son was delivered by C-section, after a

difficult labour. There were early problems establishing breastfeeding—
and then, when it was finally under way, a series of personal health problems serious enough to require hospitalization, more interruptions to the
breastfeeding, and more difficulties trying to re-establish it. "It was this
stressful exhausting thing we were trying to do," she said. "It's unfortunate
because I feel like I lost a lot, in those first three months . . . I didn't have
that initial bond with him, it didn't grow, as we kept going."

As if this wasn't enough, Gina's partner—a reluctant father from the
start—did not step in to help. When the baby was 6 months old, Gina
was offered a full-time job, and took it. She hired a "phenomenal" live-in
nanny. When we spoke, Gina was 30, and the baby was 3½. Life was much
better—but she was sure one child was all she could manage. "I'm a really
good mom to one child," she said. "I don't think I'd be a very good mom
to two."

Unlike Gina, who had always anticipated being a mother, Michelle said
that until she was approaching 30, she hadn't thought much about having
children. She was far more preoccupied with her graduate studies, and
her job. Then an emerging health concern made it a much more time-sen-
sitive question, with a "now or never" answer. She persuaded her less than
enthusiastic partner that the time had come, and got pregnant at the same
time as many of her friends. The friends seemed to be heavily into the sort
of intensive attachment parenting described in earlier chapters. Michelle
accumulated all the books ("I have a whole shelf on my bookshelf") and
thought that she would be that kind of mother too.

It didn't work out that way. "Everything was wrong" during her labour and the birth of her son—and that was just the start. Determined
to conform to what she thought she was supposed to do, she persevered
with breastfeeding, and co-slept with her son. But for two years, she felt
guilty—about not being able to be the sort of "perfect mother" she thought
her friends were modelling, and about returning to work while they were
still at home. She realized, thinking back, that she was probably suffering
from quite serious post-partum depression. There were also relationship
challenges; her partner was frequently absent because of his work, and
when he was home seemed unsympathetic to her difficulties. "I didn't
love being a mother in those first few years, and I felt guilty about that,"
she said. "The breastfeeding and the co-sleeping, I felt I had to do that
to make up for not being able to be a stay-at-home parent, and not loving
being a mom."

When we spoke, Michelle was 36, and her son Daniel was nearly 5. The passage of time had made a big difference to her thinking about second babies. For one thing, many of the friends against whom she was measuring her mothering had also returned to work. Many had also had second babies, and Michelle could see that the mothering expectations had lowered considerably. "We all loosened up," she said. Now, some of those second babies were at "that adorable toddler stage," her bond with Daniel was firm, her working life was much more secure, and her partner had become a committed and engaged father. A sibling for Daniel was now a possibility . . .

Growing the family

In giving Daniel a sibling, Michelle would be creating an entirely different kind of family. Daniel would not be the sole recipient of his parents' time and attention. A whole new complex of relationships would be introduced. And there would be much more work, both physical and emotional. So the decision to have a second baby is actually a choice of family type. And though times are changing, most parents still choose not to stop at one child. (As noted in Chapter 2, 60 percent of Canadian parents had two or more.) That was certainly the case for the parents I spoke with.

Indeed, some persevered to have the second child even when there would have been good reason to stop at one. Two mothers spoke of needing fertility treatments to conceive a second time. One mother spoke of multiple miscarriages before giving birth to her second baby. One gay couple sought a second child through the not-always-straightforward route of gestational surrogacy. Two other mothers had very similar stories to those of Gina and Diane—first babies who were difficult and demanding, fathers who were unsupportive, and depression also in the picture. But they too persevered to have a second child.

With these parents, as with most of the others I spoke to, the conversation was always about "having kids" (in the plural), with the question again being *when*, not *if*. For Simon and his wife, wanting kids meant "a minimum of two." When we talked Simon was nearly 40, and the father of three children aged 4, 2½, and 2 months. "We knew we were going to have kids, because of our age, in fairly quick succession," he said.

Issues like the availability of parental leave and other workplace concerns, finances, the availability of child-care, and perceptions of the ideal gap between children, factored in to the timing of siblings also. In most cases, there was a two- or three-year gap. Many parents in this group, dealing with a toddler and a baby, were among the busiest.

Divisions of labour, trajectories of caring

The busyness of the preschool years is worth noting again. These are the years when children need hands-on care from a constantly present care-giver. But this caregiving needs to be supported by paid employment from some source as well. It will also be clear, from the previous chapter, and from the foregoing discussion of family configurations, that there are many ways to organize the caring and the earning. There may be changes over time in how the work is divided. But early divisions of labour often play forward in particular trajectories of caring as the months and years pass. There were hints of these beginning trajectories in the families introduced in the previous chapter. Here I look more closely at some of these trajectories, and the divisions of labour that undergird them.

Not all families were readily classifiable. In one case at least, there was no-one else in the family with whom labour *could* be divided. Clive, introduced earlier, was a solo parent, depending on employment insurance in order to care full-time for his 20-month-old son. In most of the other families, however, there were two (heterosexual) parents, so my focus is on the mother-father divisions they represented.

At this early age, mothers' involvement in child-care is usually a fore-gone conclusion. There were no adoptions in this group of families; all the mothers had given birth, and were, at least in the early months, establish-ing breastfeeding. Those who had been working had taken some leave—often the full year allowed under federal legislation. So it was fathers' in-volvement in caring for their babies that was more decisive in setting up the path of care that was likely to unfold. From the accounts of the fathers I spoke with, and from reports about partners offered in my conversations with the mothers, it seemed that, in this group at least, most fathers were certainly active participants in child-care.[5]

Like Colin, introduced in the previous chapter, some of the fathers in this group had to work at being involved in those early days, especially when it was the mothers who were at home full-time, and breastfeeding as well. In those circumstances, fathers' roles seemed less clear. Committed to sharing in the pre-baby days, they were not always prepared for the fact that so much early baby care had to default to the mothers. Hélène, the mother of a 4-year-old and a 6-month-old baby, commented: "[It] threw us for a loop, because it changes the relationship or the dynamic in the family, because I was on baby care always, and that's not how we imagined it." But babies also needed to have diapers changed, and to be bathed and soothed. Mothers needed a break from babies who were unhappy or colicky. Meals needed to be prepared. Hélène's partner, and others like him, were not deterred, and took on the support work. It wasn't always easy. Ben most vividly echoed Colin's experience as he recalled his struggles to connect with an unhappy baby, who wanted only to be nursed, and who screamed for most of her first four months of life. Ben did his share of walking with her—and wryly noted that he now had permanent hearing loss in one ear. "It took me that four months to learn to love her," he said. But once the connection was made, it lasted.

Fathers as primary carers

In some cases, when mothers returned to work after a leave ended, fathers retained and sometimes expanded the caregiving involvement they had developed in the early months. Simon, introduced earlier as the father of three children, was married to a physician, who got a job across the country just after their first baby was born. The finance company Simon was working for didn't have offices in the new location, and there was no support network to help with child-care. Reluctant to move so early to non-parental care, Simon decided to try staying at home with the baby to see how it would work. Four years and two more children later, he was still at home, and planning to continue the arrangement till the most recent arrival was older. (He thought he would feel guilty not giving her the parental attention the other children had had.) He knew too that his wife's job would continue to be the privileged one. Any work that he took on in the future would have to be flexible, to accommodate her more demanding hours.

Greg had been a stay-at-home dad too, following the birth of his second child. When we spoke a third baby had arrived, and he had picked up some shifts in a retail outlet while his wife was home on parental leave. When she returned to her corporate job, he would be in charge of a 7-month-old baby, and two children in school.

In three other families, mothers were the primary earners in stable professional jobs. Fathers were working too, but in jobs that freed them to take on more of the daytime child-care. Marie's partner worked shifts, so he could be home during the day to care for their preschooler. Jamie was a graduate student, earning income as a teaching assistant with hours that gave him more time than his wife could spend with their 2-year-old. He acknowledged that some job compromises might well be in his future, with a second baby due in a few months, and a partner in a stable professional job. "I think very quickly your focus changes when you have kids," he said.

"Dual dividers": Equally sharing earning and caring

In 11 of the families I introduce here, fathers' involvement in the early months evolved to an equal sharing of caregiving when parents returned to work. In four cases, fathers had also been home full-time with babies—two on parental leave, and two because they were temporarily unemployed.

"Equal sharing" is difficult to pin down, especially in this context, and when it is based on a conversation with only one of the two parents doing the sharing. I use the term as an umbrella to cover many different circumstances in which both parents were working full-time, and also seeming to take on what looked to be a significant load of child-care as well.[6] The sharing played out differently in each family, depending on the flexibility of individual work schedules, the children involved, and the personalities and relationship dynamics of the parents.

Descriptions of "a typical day" often helped illuminate the sharing process. For example, Will's weekday started with preparing breakfast for his 3½-year-old daughter Sarah, before his wife Angela took her to day care near her workplace on her way to work. Angela did the home pick-up too, when she finished work at 5.30. Will, whose workplace was close to home, was back first and got dinner started. "So I do about 90 percent of the cooking in the house," he said. Sarah's bedtime followed fairly soon, with Angela getting her into pyjamas and brushing her teeth—"then I go up and do the books and songs." On Saturday mornings he gave Angela a break from driving by taking Sarah to her gymnastics class. The rest of the weekend was unstructured, but child-care was shared. Annette, coming to the end of a parental leave with her second baby, spoke of a partner who was able to work from home, and who had been hands-on from the beginning.

When we spoke, they were following the common sharing practice of parents in their situation—the father taking charge of the older child, while the mother spent more time with the baby. Descriptions of relationships also illuminated the sharing process. Aaron commented, "This is how our relationship works . . . She's the organizer of things, and I'm the doer of things."

In this group, changes in jobs—specifically, mothers' jobs—had already happened in two cases to keep the child-care sharing equitable. Jennifer, formerly an associate in a busy law firm, decided to open her own practice to give her more family time. Francine, a specialist nurse, gave up a demanding clinical job, for one that had more regular hours. It was a painful compromise, made, in Francine's terms, "to make it healthier for us as a family and as a couple." She added, "We've come through it. But it was a lot of fighting."

In two other families, changes in mothers' jobs were looming, prompted by the arrival of a second baby. Suzanne, the mother of a 2½-year-old, was about to go on her second maternity leave, and was considering her options when the leave ended. Returning to her job was unlikely, because of child-care costs for two children. "I would basically work to put my two children in care, which doesn't make sense," she said. Child-care costs were an issue in Ben's family, too. Ben's wife Sandy was on maternity leave with their second baby. They needed her income—Ben, a tradesman, said the family couldn't survive on his alone. But if Sandy returned to work, she (like Suzanne) would see all her earnings going to child-care. The family lived across the road from an elementary school; when I spoke with Ben, Sandy was thinking about offering before- and after-school child-care to generate some income.

Dual-earners with mothers in charge

In all the families I have introduced so far, fathers were playing an equal (and on rare occasions a greater) role in child-care than mothers. A much more common division of labour, among the families I spoke with (and one they shared with most Canadian families) was for mothers to take on more family responsibility, even if they were also working. This was the case in 11 families whose situations I consider here. In this group too, the nature of the sharing varied.

In two cases, and in contrast to the situations I have described so far, the story was not about involved fathers but rather of disengaged ones. Earlier, I introduced Gina, whose extremely difficult start to mothering resulted in the decision to have only one child, and also propelled her back to full-time work much earlier than she had planned. I noted then that her husband had been unhelpful in those early months—and so he continued to be. He did little of the hands-on "dirty work," and Gina estimated that he had not cared for their son by himself till he was 3. Lesley's story was similar. When we spoke, Lesley's two sons were 2 and 4. She commented that her husband was "not comfortable" with them as babies, and had continued to allow most caregiving responsibilities to default to her—even though both were working full-time. Part of the problem was that Lesley's job was family-friendly, and had more flexible working hours, whereas his did not. But Lesley acknowledged that the two years she had spent on two maternity leaves probably entrenched her in his eyes as the person in charge of all things family-related. "If I were to do it again . . . I would insist that there be more of that hands-on parenting when they're young," she said.

Lesley was doing all the work, as well as carrying all the responsibility. She didn't have a team. In other cases, mothers' time at home with babies, usually as solo caregivers, also led to more traditional divisions of child-care. But it was more likely to establish them as CEOs, with fathers as active field assistants. When I spoke with Beth, another lawyer, she was about to return to full-time work after her third parental leave in five years. In her case, caregiving would be shared with a supportive husband and a full-time nanny. Everyone would be busy, but Beth would be running the show. In his family, Mario, the father of two children aged 5 and 3, was that supportive husband, helping where he could in the early stages of breast-feeding, caring for the older child when the new baby came. But it was his wife who did all the research on how caregiving should be handled. "I would probably put it all on my wife as the one that did a lot of it," he said. In the case of Monica and her husband, parents of a 20-month-old, it was Monica's expertise as a teacher, with a background in child development, that made her the CEO. In the case of Paula and Rosemary, the CEO/field assistant role sharing was between two mothers. Rosemary, with the stable full-time job, was the primary earner who participated as much as she could in the care of the couple's two children. Paula described her work as a cobbling together of "a couple of gigs" to support the family income, but she was mainly responsible for child-care.

In four of the 11 families I introduce here, mothers' more prominent role in caregiving was a function of work arrangements and family finances that could accommodate their desire to work part-time. In the case of Aisha and her family, the accommodation was a challenge, and not exactly a choice. But it was something she was managing, with good humour, and with gratitude for other aspects of family life that were going well. Aisha, a Muslim immigrant from Tanzania, was working part-time as a communications consultant in the mornings. Her partner, still part-way through graduate studies, worked full-time afternoon and evening shifts at a big-box store. So their child-care—for two children aged 4½ and nearly 2—was also in shifts. The arrangement gave Aisha most time with the children. But she noted the cultural shift that her husband's involvement signalled. "If we lived in Tanzania, I highly doubt that he would give the kids a bath, or cook, but he does all that here," she said. "I leave at 7. And when I come back at 1 . . . everything's done. The only difference is the decision-making. I make most of the decisions, when it comes to our children, because I feel like I know more, I spend more time reading."

Jane (a nurse), Penny (a geologist), and Fiona (a school psychologist) were all able to do professional work in organizations that were amenable to part-time hours, with the support of partners in full-time employment. In all three cases, part-time work was a choice made to ease the stress of family life and household management when both parents are employed full time, and they were aware of their privilege in being able to make it. Leo, a teacher, and his husband Mitch were two fathers in the same position. Leo, like Jane, Penny, and Fiona, was able to work part-time in order to take on the family responsibilities.

Mothers at home

The most traditional division of labour, and one that is diminishing in prominence in Canada, sees mothers at home as primary carers, with fathers as primary earners. Ten families followed this model—though the arrangement was pragmatic, not ideological, in several of them. This was nowhere more clear than in the case of Hugh, a father of two children aged 2½ and 6 months. Hugh's wife was at home with their children mainly because, for this family as for many others already noted, child-care costs would consume all of the second income. So Hugh was the primary earner—but he was also as involved as he could possibly be in his children's care outside of work. He didn't know about the availability of parental leave for fathers when his first child was born, but took three months with his second. "It may well be the best three months of my entire life," he said. Hugh's job was to drive a delivery truck; he had an mp3 player on board, and liked to listen to talks and lectures by parenting experts while he was driving. "It's fantastic," he said. "I spend all day at work learning to be a dad so I can come home and apply it. I've learned so much by just going to work and listening."

In fact, in four of the families in which mothers were at home full-time, it was the fathers I spoke with. But fathers' involvement came up in conversations with some of the at-home mothers as well. I introduced Karen earlier as the older mother of just one child, her daughter Ellie. Karen said that, from the outside, she and her husband John probably looked like a 1950s household. "But, he gets home after a long, sometimes miserable day . . . and it's 100 percent about her," she said. "I don't get him until bedtime."

This was not always the case. Nicole's shift to at-home motherhood came after her second child was born. Before that, she had been working as an engineer. There had been a very difficult maternity leave with her first baby (another situation where the father was disengaged—and also critical of housework not done), and a return to paid work which was "awful." Tired of long working days and 11 hours of daycare for her baby, she decided that this was "not the kind of parent I wanted to be." So she didn't return to work when her second baby was born. When we spoke, the children were 5 and 18 months old, and Nicole continued to struggle, with little support from her husband and not much from any other source.

Regarding the other mother-at-home families, two scenarios need to be mentioned. The first relates to ideas about families—perhaps "family values" is the lens to use. None of the families I have introduced to date had more than three children. Kate, however, was the mother of five, aged between 7 years and 2 months. Kate lived in a Nova Scotia community where church affiliation was strong, and large families were much more common. Kate's family resembled those of a couple of generations ago—and as I will point out later, it shared some of the child-rearing advantages of those earlier times. Of course it also placed heavy demands on Kate. But perhaps not surprisingly, she felt her situation was freely chosen, and she relished her role as a full-time mother. When we spoke, she was also home-schooling the two oldest children.

The second scenario, and one in which heavy demands are also placed on mothers, links more explicitly to a style of child-rearing which is intensively child-centred. "Attachment parenting" (described in Chapter 1 as one of the popular but contentious models confronting contemporary parents) is taken up to some extent in many families, but some of its key tenets (like extended breastfeeding, and co-sleeping with children till they are ready to sleep alone) are hard to implement fully unless the mother is available on an ongoing basis. A commitment to this style of parenting was what kept mothers like Heather at home.

In conclusion . . .

This chapter has focused on two critical elements in the care of children during the preschool years: the size of the family, and the way the caring work is divided. Parents' decisions about the number of children they want, as I noted earlier, come down to a choice of family style, with radically different implications in terms of care demands and children's experiences. How the caring work is divided has implications too. From the foregoing, it's clear that gender was an important factor in the way hands-on care, and overall responsibility for family life, was shared during these early years. But it's also clear that conventional understandings of mothering and fathering were being disrupted—as families faced real-life situations that demanded pragmatic and sometimes non-traditional responses, and as fathers, as well as mothers, discovered the transformative effects of caring for their little ones. Also significant, it must be said, were the situations where conventional gender understandings were *not* disrupted, and mothers were unduly burdened.

With the background this chapter has provided, it's now possible to look more closely at the *detail* of child-rearing in the preschool years. In the next chapter I look at the decisions parents are making, the strategies they are trying out, and the context in which all this work is being done.

5

Preschoolers and the work of care

The divisions of labour and the trajectories of care described in the previous chapter are an important part of the context in which decisions about caregiving (on a daily basis) and child-rearing (in the longer term) are made. This chapter digs deeper into the realities for parents of caring for children in the preschool years—what they decide to do (and how they decide) at various stages of their children's development, what sort of support they get, what challenges they face, how they cope. And since the children concerned are now a little older, I pay some attention to them too, not as mere recipients of care, but as individuals interacting with the people caring for them, and experiencing the world in particular and sometimes unanticipated ways.

The big decisions

No two parents, and no two children, are alike. Child-rearing is different in different families. But some of the key differences play out in two areas that cast long shadows across the preschool years: parents' approaches to children's sleep, and the extent to which they encourage their children's independence. A third area, closely linked to perspectives on independence, is parents' management of children's time.

Seeking sleep

I start with a discussion of children's sleep because it is a critical preoccupation for almost all parents with children in this age group. It is also an issue that invites different approaches, which tend to align with different parenting styles and philosophies.

The first approach relates to the "attachment parenting" described in Chapter 1. I noted there the basic tenets—extended breastfeeding, close physical contact, and having the baby sleep in (or very close to) the parents' bed until s/he is ready for a solo sleeping arrangement. Fundamental to this approach—at least in its "purest" form—is that babies are not left to cry. If parents decide to follow the tenets of attachment parenting, they may be committing to co-sleeping with their children, perhaps for longer periods than they may have anticipated. If they don't, they are probably committing to the sometimes emotionally challenging alternative approach of "sleep training," also described in Chapter 1, which involves settling babies in their own beds once they reach five or six months. With this approach, parents are instructed to develop a warm, loving, consistent bedtime routine, and then put the baby down to sleep while s/he is awake. The core of sleep training is to leave the baby—initially just a moment or two, and then for longer—before going back to check and comfort. As I noted then, it's a contentious and divisive issue which tends, at least in its online manifestations, to place parents in different camps; in deciding what to do about sleep, parents are also pushed to choose between an approach to child-rearing that is explicitly child-centred, and one that, in contrast, acknowledges the needs of parents too.

The practice of co-sleeping is common in other cultures, as mothers introduced in earlier chapters have pointed out. Patricia's Chinese mother and grandmother both followed it. Aisha, growing up in Tanzania, slept on the same bed with her single mother till she was 17. "How you're raised plays a huge role," she said. "That's what I was used to, that's what many families do, in that culture." Jessica described parenting approaches in her native Korea:

> The first thing is the sleep training. Then letting kids explore things by themselves. They never let them, they sleep with them till they are about seven years old. I still remember I slept with my mom. My friends in Korea sleep with their kids.

The difference in countries like Canada is that, as noted in Chapter 1, co-sleeping (because of its reported association with Sudden Infant Death Syndrome, or SIDS) runs counter to all the official advice parents are given. And co-sleeping over an extended period with children who don't settle well is perhaps more difficult to sustain when both parents are employed outside the home, and usually have to manage with very little other household support. Getting up and going to work is hard enough in busy dual-earner households with preschoolers. Sleep deprivation makes it even harder.

Heather was one of the stay-at-home mothers I introduced in the previous chapter. When we met, Heather's son was 2½, and her daughter was 4 months old. Heather was practising attachment parenting in its "pure" form. She had been at home full-time since the birth of her son. She was breastfeeding the baby, and continuing to nurse her son occasionally too. Both children were sleeping with their parents, in an arrangement that involved a king-sized mattress on the bedroom floor, and a twin mattress beside it. Heather's husband slept on the twin mattress, and Heather slept on the king-sized one with a child on either side of her. They had tried to move their son to his own bed many times, but he always woke up, and got "very worked up." "It's not like we haven't tried, but we've never pushed it," Heather said. "He will do it when he's ready."

Marie, the mother of 4½-year-old Charlie, was also a passionate advocate of attachment parenting. Like Heather, she was continuing to breastfeed, at bedtime and first thing in the morning, because she thought it should be Charlie's choice to decide when to wean. When we spoke, Charlie was almost at that point:

> And I have struggled a lot, because although I believe in this, it's not always comfortable or convenient, and I know there's a lot of people who judge, right? So I would have much preferred that it had stopped sooner. But I feel proud that we have gotten to the point where we made it his call.

The decision to end co-sleeping would also be Charlie's call, though in Marie's judgment the practice worked as well for his parents as it did for Charlie, since their sleep was not disturbed by getting up to attend to him. The family was about to move house. They planned to make a big occasion of setting up a special room for Charlie, with a special bed of his own, and hoped that would be an end to the co-sleeping.

If Heather and Marie exemplified one approach to parenting preschoolers, Simon, introduced earlier as the stay-at-home father of three children, represented another. He didn't hesitate when I asked him about attachment parenting and co-sleeping. "Oh no, none of that!" he said. "If you have multiple kids, are you going to have them all in your bed?" The alternative—children going to sleep in their own beds, and staying asleep—requires at least some version of the "sleep training" described above. That's what Simon, and many of the other parents of preschoolers practised—to the extent that their children needed "training." Some children, as their parents thankfully noted, were just good sleepers, who after a few months started to sleep through the night on their own without any special effort on their parents' part. In other cases, especially involving babies accustomed to night-time nursing, it took some work, and a commitment on the part of parents to let them cry at least a little bit. Simon's children were disposed fairly early to sleep through the night, so the sleep training worked well. "We're quite spoiled that our kids kind of crash, and don't require any real craziness to go to sleep," he said.

Other parents used sleep training because they took seriously the official warning that co-sleeping increased the risk of SIDS. Still others, especially those in dual-earner families, also felt a need to be practical, and to train their children to sleep through the night so that they themselves could sleep. "I am a person who needs my sleep," Suzanne said. "I value my sleep and I am not a happy person without my sleep." From my conversations with all the preschooler parents, it seemed that fathers often took the sleep-training lead—often also with the interests of mothers in mind. Will wanted to protect a wife still suffering from some post-partum distress. Mark's wife was more sympathetic to attachment parenting, but he was concerned that, pregnant with their second child, she needed to be getting more sleep. It was also fathers, rather than mothers, who spoke about the sleep training of children as important to partner relationships. "Fran and I still want to be husband and wife," said Stephen. Trevor, the father of a 4-year-old and a one-year-old, commented that he and his wife Carol still needed some space to themselves. "Carol's biggest complaint is that there's always somebody holding her . . . She needs to recharge a little bit, having nobody around."

How parents ultimately decided which approach to follow was another question. Heather and Marie belonged to an online attachment parenting group which both found valuable, and which seemed to have guided their thinking from the start. Simon's wife learned about sleep training from a co-worker, and from another friend who recommended a book. Others consulted sleep training websites, hired sleep consultants, or borrowed information from friends who had done so. But in many cases, ideas changed as they came into contact with actual children.

If there was one resounding message that emerged from my conversations with parents of preschoolers, it was the need to do what worked—in individual and sometimes changing family circumstances, and with children who were uniquely themselves. Approaches that seemed attractive in theory often failed in practice, and approaches that worked splendidly with the first child often did not suit the second. So parents' practices evident in the preschool years were not nearly as fixed as the foregoing may have suggested. And the shifts in thinking and the changes of mind worked in many directions. Michelle, the unhappy mother introduced in the previous chapter, who co-slept out of a sense of duty with her first child, was resolved that it wouldn't happen with a second child. Hélène, persuaded by her online research that attachment parenting was what she would try with her first baby, changed her mind when "real life happened," and neither she nor the baby were getting any sleep. Francine, diffident about sleep training because it meant letting a baby cry, came to feel that as her babies got older they became "little people" who would be well able to handle some detachment. Annette, anxious about many things (including the risk of SIDS) with her first baby, was much more relaxed with her second—and found that co-sleeping was actually much easier on her than getting up to attend to a baby sleeping elsewhere. Francine said, "At some point I really did overkill, in terms of information. And with time I realized it's about fit, there's no theory that will work with my child. My child is very different than other children, so it's what works for us."

But if parents ended up concluding that they just needed to find what worked to get their children to sleep through the night, many were still searching at the time I spoke with them. There seemed to be very few families in this group in which everyone, most of the time, was getting a good night's sleep . . .

Tumbles, risks and independence

Heather, whose approach to her children's sleep was described above, seemed to extend a similar care and protectiveness to her 2½-year-old when it came to the inevitable tumbles and scrapes of the early years. Tumbles were going to happen, she said. But she thought her response might be different from some other parents in that "if he falls down, and cries, I'm going to comfort him":

I don't think I'm spoiling him, by comforting him if he's hurt. I don't say to him, "Oh, it's not that bad, you're fine." I hear that a lot from my mom, and mother-in-law, and grandpa, when they're here, "You're fine, you're fine." I don't want to baby him, but I also don't feel like he needs to toughen up right now.

Simon, matter-of-fact about sleep training his children, didn't want them coddled either. The two older children, aged 4 and 2½, played alone in the backyard (watched by Simon as he worked in the kitchen). At least partly because there were three children in the family under 5, he thought it was important that they learn to be as self-sufficient as possible. So the 4-year-old was expected to "clean up when she's done making a mess." She dressed herself, in the mornings, and at bedtime. She also helped her dad, by rinsing the dishes after dinner, by helping in the kitchen—even chopping with a dull knife. He liked to let her try things.

In my comparisons of Heather and Simon, the parallels between their different approaches to attachment and sleep, and their views on children's independence, can only be taken so far. Many factors, like their gender, and the number and ages of their children, could play into the different parenting approaches each seemed to represent. But their differences did indicate the range of thinking and practice that emerged from my conversations with the parents of preschoolers about their tolerance of risk where their children were concerned, and their thoughts on children's independence.

Keeping children close at night did not always link to daytime practices. Most parents were aware of the now widely publicized concerns about "helicopter parenting." Parents of children at the younger end of the age range generally announced their *intention* not to hover, or to rush in after a tumble that seemed minor. In the very early preschool years, it was sometimes too early for intention to have translated into practice. In other cases, though, even when children were still very young, it was possible to distinguish some parents who seemed more protective from some who were more willing to consider freedom and risk-taking as steps to their children's independence.

Fiona, the mother of a 4-year-old and a 2-year-old, was on the more protective side. She spoke of getting outside with her children as much as possible—but they were not left unsupervised in their backyard. Though she was more relaxed about bumps and bruises with her second than she had been with her first, hospital visits and broken bones were a lingering fear. At the park, she watched other parents, to see what they were willing to let their children do . . .

Kyle, in contrast, was a parent who was definitely willing to allow some risk. The day before we spoke, he had taken his 2-year-old daughter snowboarding. She knew it was a hobby of his, and she had been asking about it. Kyle commented that his daughter was very active, and agile—"and she does fall." On those occasions, he usually let her get up on her own. He encouraged her independence in other ways too. "Growing up in a really urban environment, I'm not scared," he said. "I let her walk around everywhere." In grocery stores, and other places they visited, she interacted with many adults. "I don't want her to feel uncomfortable in situations like that," he said. "Obviously I'm protective of her, [but] we don't want to be overprotective." Suzanne, the mother of Thea, another adventurous 2-year-old, felt the same way. Thea now spent more time at the park climbing rocks than playing on the equipment. Inside the house there was a crib mattress set up so she could launch herself on to it from the living room chairs.

Leo, the father of a 3-year-old and a one-year-old, brought his experience as an elementary school teacher to his thinking about the independence of his own children. "I think especially as a teacher I've seen a lot of overly attached kids and I don't want my [kids] to be that way," he said. So cuts and bruises were a part of life for the 3-year-old. "I know that if he needs me he will seek me. And what I've noticed is that he does fall a lot. Eighty percent of the time, he just gets right back up and keeps on going. It's the twenty percent that he actually needs me." Leo had many practical strategies, learned on the job, for dealing with the 20-percent occasions. He added: "My philosophy of parenting is, I need to get them ready for the world. The world does not start when they're adults. The world starts now."

That was Samantha's thinking too. Perhaps more clearly than any of the other parents, she articulated not only a belief in the importance of teaching children how to be responsible for themselves, but also her faith in their ability to do so. Samantha and her husband Don were the parents of 5-year-old twins—and the fact that there were two children at the same developmental stage who were constantly together of course made a difference to all the parental decisions. The twins, aged about 2, had learned to ride balance bikes. When they were 3, they got their first pedal bikes. When Samantha and I spoke, their father had set up stunts in the yard for them to ride over. They were allowed to climb on playground equipment to the level they felt comfortable—knowing they wouldn't get any help if they got stuck. They were always "fiercely proud" of their accomplishments. "[F]rom when they were very little, they've impressed me with what they were capable of," Samantha said. "I just had no idea kids were so capable, I didn't . . . I am just delighted by every little step towards independence that they enjoy taking. And they're very capable." Penny agreed. Her nearly-5-year-old son lived in a city residential neighbourhood—but one day a week he attended a forest school, one of a growing number in Canada, aimed at giving children ongoing access to a natural outdoor environment.[1] His father had bought him a pocket knife, and taught him how to use it . . .

In the foregoing, I have indicated the main approaches to the question of children's risk-taking, and the related question of their independence. But causes and correlations are hard to pin down. From their own accounts, and those of their partners, fathers overall were somewhat more willing to stand back and let tumbles happen. But there were also fathers in the group whose protectiveness seemed to be a big part of their identity as fathers. (Bruce, the father of a 2-year-old daughter, commented, "I am way more of a hover parent than my wife is. . . My wife will be the one to tell me to back off and let her play. And I'm the one who's ready to jump in and rescue!") There were also differences in children. Many parents commented on children who were either active and adventurous, or seemingly risk-averse themselves. The number and ages of children in a family made a difference too; siblings close in age sometimes had more autonomy than only children. And as I will discuss in more detail shortly, where families lived also affected parents' thinking about risk and children's independence. These and many other factors helped determine the paths parents seemed to be following.

Children's time use

Giving children some independence means, in many situations, standing back and letting them experience the world around them on their own terms, without intrusive supervision. That was clearly the thinking behind some of the approaches just noted. When it came to children's time use, the balance for most parents was between the sort of unstructured free play Suzanne's daughter was enjoying in the park, and the more structured activities, always requiring adult supervision, that were also options in this age group. Parents were always concerned about what their children were learning—and the need for them to learn (readiness for kindergarten came up in several conversations). There was an implicit understanding, perhaps linked to the widespread stress on development in the early years noted in earlier chapters, that children needed to be stimulated. But there were some differences in thinking about the form that stimulation might take. Those who seemed most keen on free play were aware of what children could learn from it, both cognitively and socially. Leo and Simon both had stories of curious children pushing to learn for themselves what other parents thought could best be taught in formal settings. (In both cases, the examples they gave was of learning starting with children writing their own names, then requesting information about the letters in other people's names . . .)

Thinking about children's learning shaped—and was shaped by—the places where they were spending most of their daytime hours. More than half of the preschool children whose parents I spoke with needed some outside child-care, and the split between day homes in the community, and institutional day-care centres, was about equal. Choices were constrained by cost and availability, and also the age and temperament of the child. Will and his wife, dual-earners and parents of 3½-year-old Sarah, were strongly in the not-hovering, free-play camp. They registered Sarah in a day home which seemed to offer almost entirely unstructured play. There was little TV watching, few electronic toys, and a big backyard with a lot of outdoor play materials. Will's explanation for their choice covered a lot of ground:

> She's a pretty energetic kid, but she's also pretty introverted sometimes, and I feel like putting her all day in a space with 20 or 30 kids, I don't know . . . I'm not in a huge rush. A lot of our friends are, "Oh, I want to make sure my kids are challenged, so they're ready for preschool, and they're learning to read." I'm much more concerned with Sarah being happy and just learning how to learn, being curious . . .

Stephen and his wife made a similar choice for their 2-year-old. They registered her in a day home run by an award-winning child-care worker, who warned them, "She's going to be dirty!" ("And we were like, we love it!" Stephen said.) Other parents, as Will noted, did favour institutional day care settings on the assumption that they would be more structured and (therefore) more appropriate for kindergarten preparation. Francine's daughter was in a day home till she was 3, then moved to an institutional day-care centre with more organized activities. Jennifer started her son in a day care centre (where she thought he would "learn stuff"), then moved him at 3 to a more structured program which would be "more challenging, more interesting."

Most parents took advantage of local community programs for pre-schoolers, like storytime and music sessions at the library, or swimming at the pool, though there were differences in take-up depending on parents' work situations. Greg's 6-year-old had a piano lesson once a week, and he and his nearly 5-year-old brother took karate lessons—offered just down the street, and on a fairly casual basis. Greg worked part-time in a dual-earner household; he said they tried not to do too much so there was still family time, and routines like the weekly visit to the farmers' market. For parents in full-time jobs, there was little time left for extra commitments, and the children of those parents, in a variety of child-care settings during the day, may also have been glad to get home and stay home. Children of parents who were home-based were in a different space, with parents themselves needing to provide what structure they thought was necessary. Karen, at home with a 4-year-old, chose a few structured activities every week—two pre-school sessions, a playgroup, or a library program, a playdate at the zoo or at home. There was also time set aside for reading and time for imaginative play.

In this age group, screen time was starting to emerge as a concern, with most parents aware that it would become a much more complicated matter as their children got older. Here too, there were different opinions. In some households, there were strict rules. Francine's children (a 6-year-old and a 3-year-old) had access to television and other family technology only on weekends. Mark's son Adam, at 2½, watched favourite children's shows that were streamed in 10-minute segments, without commercials, and timed to fit with a particular activity. (When Mark and I spoke, Adam was eating lunch and watching an episode of a current preschooler favourite, "Paw Patrol.") Mark was a systems analyst, with strong views on the need for children to understand computer technology. In the next few months, he planned to give Adam an old device with some games on it. Later, he would teach Adam how to code . . .

Most households fitted somewhere in between these two positions. Children watched some shows, on television screens or tablets, when their parents needed time for other responsibilities—getting ready for work in the morning, or preparing dinner in the evening. But parents' talk about children's screen time usually also included comments about the need to monitor it—and in some cases also, their guilt about making use of it as an easy way to keep children entertained. Until a couple of months before I met her, Monica's 20-month-old son Drew had had no screen time. Then his parents took him on a lengthy road trip—and gave him an iPad for entertainment during the drive. "Now I'd say—this is my mom guilt moment—he watches a cartoon in the car every time we're in the car," Monica said. "And I felt really guilty about it. And then I thought, after work, I need that quiet time. And I think Drew needs that quiet time, even just in the car, where he's just zoning out." Trevor's 4-year-old watched some TV. "I think, well, some of it's educational, just kids' program stuff," he said. "But I also think, like, as an adult, what do adults do? They watch TV, they work in front of screens too. Still finding the balance there."

Gathering information

On all the issues discussed so far, parents are not acting in a vacuum. As earlier chapters have pointed out, Canadian parents are raising their children in a particular social and cultural context in which messages about what they *should* be doing are both pervasive and mixed. Among the parents I spoke with, there was certainly an awareness of the messages, which they encountered through many sources. Asked where she got her information, Heather said, "Online. Obviously." As noted earlier, she and several other mothers I spoke with belonged to an online attachment parenting group. Those who tried sleep training used books, consulted websites, hired sleep consultants (or borrowed material from friends who had). Other reading included posts on Facebook groups for parents, or parenting blogs, or newspaper or magazine articles posted through social media. Books about parenting issues were also mentioned—though there were comments too about the fact that reading books took time that wasn't always available. Asked to describe her information sources, Fiona said, "I think a little bit of everything. Because I was looking for answers."

From their own accounts, and those of their partners, mothers tended to be more engaged. Trevor said his wife, now a home-based mother with a professional background in psychology and work with children, made information-gathering a job. "She's kind of a workaholic," he said. "So without being in a workplace she had kind of taken a role of really reading and digesting so much more information on child development and stuff." Stephen commented that his wife definitely did more research than he did, "to the point where, she should do less research, she gets caught up in it too much, I find."

While many fathers did leave most of the information-gathering to their partners, some were readers too. In several families information-gathering was a joint enterprise. There were many comments about the need to sift through conflicting positions on a variety of issues, and either, in Bruce's terms, look for "the common-sense middle ground," or check their findings with someone they trusted in the real world. Bruce described himself as a "lifelong IT guy." He was sharply critical of the effect of communications technology on parents seeking information. "It's caustic," he said. "It's a terrible environment."

Mothers were aware of the environment also. In general, they either followed sources whose opinions tended to coincide with their own (like those committed to attachment parenting, for example) or they looked only for information on specific, short-term problems. Jessica's example was about treating a fever in her 16-month-old. Aisha joked that she sometimes consulted "Dr. Google."

The two mothers introduced in the previous chapter, whose early experiences had been particularly painful, also were the most dismissive of online material. Gina said she and her husband made a pact not to consult the internet about how to parent their son, now 3½. "There are so many things, and no-one is right or wrong," she said. "But I could get myself so over-the-top concerned—a cut on his foot is all of a sudden gangrene." Michelle, the mother of the nearly-5-year-old, said she now had little time for parenting websites. Once in a while, she said, she might look at a Facebook post. But the ones she preferred were the ones written by women who were being "totally honest about how shitty it is to be a parent sometimes."

Finding support

Many parents were well aware of the down-side of going online in search of information. But they also took advantage of the social media up side—the ability to connect, not only with like-minded individuals in Facebook-type groups, but also with friends and family who lived far away. There were many examples, but two in particular are interesting contrasts. Jane was in a group text with her two best friends, who were raising children in other cities. Jane said they texted every day, on "everything from 'I'm having a terrible day, the baby was up all night' to . . . what do you do about this?'" In Jane's case, her social media connections were only a part of the support she could draw on. When her first child, now 6, was a baby she and her husband moved back to the town where they grew up. Her mother-in-law, a devoted grandmother, babysat during Jane's part-time work shifts. Other family members and old friends were also around. Every week, there was usually a coffee date at someone's house. Five or six mothers came and brought their children.

Diane, raising a 3-year-old in a country town far away from her family, talked online to her mother and sister every day. "Thank goodness for things like Skype and videochat, because otherwise we would be extremely isolated," she said. "It's a really important part of our support system."

Most parents had social media connections of some kind to keep in touch with friends and family, and those connections were often very important to them. But the difference between people like Jane, who also had plenty of concrete support on the ground, and Diane, who had none, was significant. Virtual support was some compensation, but it could not entirely replace what real people, close at hand, could offer. The most fundamental support most parents expect is from their partners, and I have described in the previous chapter the cases, rare in this group of families, where partner support was lacking. But aside from partners, among all the parents I spoke with, it was the presence of grandparents that made the biggest difference.

Trevor, his wife Carol and their children lived across the road from Carol's parents. "Grandma comes over, and she helps all the time," Trevor said.

> Grandpa is around to help too. But specifically Grandma has just been like—I don't know how we could have done it without her being around. Just, emotional support, helping to take care of the kids, helping to cook sometimes. It's been fantastic.

Grandparents were not always an unqualified blessing. In a few families, there were tensions. But in this group grandparents provided much-appreciated help of some kind in about half the families. Those who lived close at hand, especially if they weren't themselves employed, were reported as offering regular babysitting. Distant grandparents came for long visits, often at critical times when their help was most needed. Working grandparents took grandchildren on weekends, and provided meals. Above all, they were the people parents could call on in an emergency, without a second thought.

A few other families described other kinds of support they could depend on. Will and his wife shared their home with a close friend, who was a surrogate aunt to their daughter. A mother-daughter duo in a neighbouring apartment provided ongoing back-up for Ben and his wife, parents of children aged 3½ and 8 months. Leo's widowed and childless aunt came to live near Leo and his partner Mitch and their two young children, to be a support for them. Another same-sex couple, Paula and Rosemary, lived a province away from their families, but in the city they moved to they found a supportive queer community, with members well aware of the need to "be there" for others. Jessica, missing her mother in Korea, counted on her friends, and also on the Sure Start program offered as a parent resource in her British Columbia community; she visited its drop-in play space nearly every week day. Clive, the single father on Employment Insurance in order to care full-time for his 20-month-old, also made daily use of a parent resource centre—in his case almost his only support. Bruce described a tight network of friends that had developed before children arrived, and had simply expanded to embrace them. Annette named some good friends, a former nanny, and their dayhome provider, who lived next door. "It's a bit tough not having family around, but we manage," she said. Many other families were managing too—but feeling that for practical purposes they were managing on their own.

Two themes emerged from my conversations with parents about support. The first was that it was family support they counted on, and missed when it was not available. The second was that, in spite of the social connections and support that friends could offer, it was usually a different kind of support. Friends could not so readily be asked to pitch in with practical help when daily life with little ones was particularly overwhelming. My sense was that this reluctance was partly based on parents' unwillingness to impose on people who were likely to be as stressed and busy as they were themselves. But it was also in some cases based on a feeling that to ask for help was to declare oneself in some way less than capable as a parent. Friends—especially newer, post-baby friends—could be supportive, but they could also judge. And from another angle, anxious parents, mothers in particular, were sometimes unwilling to trust their babies to anyone else. Heather spoke of a more general lack of support for people raising children. "Society doesn't feel accommodating sometimes to parents, and then that leaves us isolated," she said. "It leaves parents having to do it all. And it is so hard. Even though you love [your children] so much, you get so worn down."

Children and community

Isolation and a lack of social support hardly described the experience of Samantha and her partner, raising their twins on one of British Columbia's Gulf Islands. "This community is profoundly supportive," Samantha said. "And there are a number of local traditions in place beyond people's inherent community-mindedness and generosity." (One of the traditions, with the arrival of a baby, was a roster set up to provide a month of meals.) The community was small enough that people knew each other. There was always someone willing to hold a baby in a grocery store while a parent paid at the till. "Nobody looks at you here like, 'Oh, your children are too noisy,'" Samantha said. She was part of a parenting group at the school, attended by about 20 other parents with children of all ages—"another fantastic resource".

The community as a physical space—and the space Samantha's family occupied within it—also played a significant role in the way the children were being raised. The twins' bike-riding independence, noted earlier, was possible in a community with safe bike trails, and a home property close to trees and a beach, where the twins could spend hours outside. There were some disadvantages—there were no conventional sources of outdoor recreation, like swimming pools, or gyms. But for Samantha they were far outweighed by the advantages. "I can't imagine a better place to be a parent, in many ways," she said.

Living in a friendly but geographically isolated island community would be neither possible nor appealing for most parents. But elements of the experience Samantha and her family enjoyed would certainly resonate with some. Most of the parents I spoke with lived in residential neighbourhoods in urban centres, which came with a different set of possibilities and constraints. In most cases, they were also different from the neighbourhoods in which many had grown up. Beth remembered living as a child in an immigrant family, in a neighbourhood where there were other immigrant families, and lots of children. She articulated a common experience: "I could go outside, without any parental supervision . . . Just ride my bike around and come home when the street lights came on. And if my parents weren't home after school, I could just go to the neighbour's house." Beth now lived with her husband and three children (aged 5, 3, and 10 months) in a Toronto neighbourhood. They barely knew the neighbours on either side. The children were not allowed to play in the front yard. "So, the neighbourhood feel isn't there, as much," she said. "And I feel like I'm doing a lot more supervision of my children than maybe I got . . . I definitely feel like we are supervising the kids a lot more."

Beth's situation was, not surprisingly, much more common than Samantha's. The sort of extensive supervision of children that Beth was undertaking might seem inevitable in environments where neighbours are not known, and among the parents of preschoolers I spoke with, this was often the case. Some parents were particularly confined. Aisha and her husband lived with two children under 5 in an apartment. They depended on a park nearby or on indoor playgrounds available in the community to give their children some play space away from home, as well as providing interaction. Hugh and his wife, with two children under 3, were also apartment-dwellers. Their children's experience of life outside home was based mainly on the Ontario Early Years program offered in the community and on family connections through their church. They hoped to go camping this year, when admission to the national parks was free, to give their children a different outdoor experience.

But even families like Beth's—living in homes in residential neighbourhoods—experienced some constraints. Neighbourhoods differed in their location, design, and resident population, and each of these elements affected parents' choices and children's freedom. Both Aaron and Eliot, living in Vancouver, commented on the fact that there were few white families in their neighbourhoods. Both implied that cultural differences impeded contact. Bruce, in Calgary, described the trade-off he and his wife made, between a house with an established yard in an older neighbourhood, and one in a new city suburb (the choice of many of their friends). The yard was important to Bruce—but there were no children around. He thought there might have been a stronger sense of community in one of the newer suburbs. Lesley, another Calgary parent, lived in a suburb where all the neighbours had grown children. Lesley reported that they seemed "thrilled" to have little kids living on their street again—but the little kids in question had no playmates close at hand.

Dennis and his wife and 2½-year-old lived on a quiet street in a neighbourhood with "lots of kids." In the summers, walking by, they'd stop and
chat to neighbours, but at this early stage, none were close friends. Asked
how he would feel about letting his daughter cross the street to visit friends
or walk to the park nearby he said, "I'd have to feel it out, when it's appropriate, but absolutely." Will, with a 3½-year-old, was similarly confident
about future possibilities. The family lived in a neighbourhood with many
young families, and near a park, where he had seen kids he thought were
about 9 playing together without parents around. He would "absolutely"
like his daughter to have that freedom. What both he and Dennis would
have to do, though, was make an effort to get to know the neighbours, and
to create the "neighbourhood feel" that Beth recalled.

That's what Trevor was trying to do. His comments about neighbours
and community drew many threads together:

> I don't know a lot of parents in the area. I've seen them. But I'm
> hoping—and again, us being introverts, we don't necessarily get out
> there so much. But Carol [his wife] has met lots of people at the
> preschool. I've also met some of them too. But I'm hoping—and the
> older I get I think the more extroverted I get—I'll take the chance to
> talk to people. So I'm actually looking forward to running into par-
> ents at the school, and seeing them, and then seeing them around
> the neighbourhood. Because right now I don't necessarily . . .

Some mothers were a few steps ahead on Trevor's path. Karen, the
home-based mother of a 4-year-old, had met other mothers through visits
to the local park. She thought her neighbourhood was fairly "free-range,"
perhaps facilitated by its design. "We have a lot of cul de sacs," she said.
"So on the cul de sacs, there are definitely the moms who say, 'Stay on the
cul de sac. If cars come by, get out of the way.' And they [the moms] might
be at the window or in the yard." Freedom certainly wouldn't extend to
letting children go to a big park some distance from home, and "wander
around at age five." But, for Karen, it would extend to letting her daughter
walk to a friend's house, a block away, while she stood on the sidewalk near
her house and watched.

Paula, living with her partner and two children in a quiet older neighbourhood in another city, described a real-life experience along the lines
Karen was imagining:

A couple of weeks ago I let a 7-year-old and a 5-year-old take James [her 4½-year-old] to a park a block away. We'd never done that before. And the mom [of the other children] said this was something new that she was doing too. And she stood at the corner and watched them go back and forth to the park a couple of times. And I said, OK, if you can be responsible for James, then you can take him to the park. They went to the park and they only stayed a few minutes, and then they came back. It involved crossing a road . . . I was really excited about that.

So much seemed to come down to the individual neighbourhood, and what might be possible when children were a little older. Francine lived in an intensely urban neighbourhood in Montreal with her partner, plus a 6-year-old daughter and a 3-year-old son. The 6-year-old, like most of the other neighbourhood children, was at the local public school. "Now we are starting to develop a network of parents that watch out for each other's kids because we all know the kids, because they are all in school," she said. That network wasn't available when the children were younger. "But now it's starting to develop, and also our kids are a bit more independent. I don't let my daughter go out without any kind of supervision, but I think it will come." I asked what that first unsupervised step might be. Francine thought it might be a trip to buy something at the local bakery. The bakery would be a safe starting point. Because their children were at school together, she knew the baker . . .

Francine's community was not as intentional or as extensive as Samantha's island community was. But it was a much closer approximation than anything most of the other parents experienced. It was hard not to be struck, in many stories, by the parental watchfulness and caution that accompanied children's encounters with the world outside their front doors. So many parents did not really know their neighbours, and without that connection, did not feel able to ease up on the supervision of their children outside. And Hélène pointed out the problem of neighbourhoods with few children. "If I wanted to send my kids out on the street, there are no kids on the street, there's no safety in numbers," she said. Hélène would have liked a "free-range" neighbourhood with many children. Her strategy to replace it was to get together with friends, and find spaces—in one another's homes, on trips to the park, or the country, where "kids can disappear." A privileged few, like Mark and Annette, in Ontario, had access to cottages where their children were more free to explore outside. But special arrangements, and special occasions, did not cover daily life.

When many parents, and their children, spend most of their time—at work, or in child-care—outside the neighbourhoods where they live, it could be argued that it doesn't matter whether those neighbourhoods are actual, viable communities—what were described in Chapter 2 as "communities of place." There are two powerful counter-arguments. The first is that if children need to be driven or otherwise escorted everywhere they go—usually to be supervised in another location—they have very little autonomy. The second counter-argument is that the absence of neighbourly sociability and contact between adults and children on a daily basis produces an environment ripe for anonymous surveillance—the sort of surveillance so perfectly illuminated by the case of the Winnipeg mother and her children, described in earlier chapters.

(More) challenges and concerns

Surveillance, in fact, could be counted as one of the major challenges for this group of parents. The surveillance to which parents are subjected always purports to come with children's best interests in mind, and links directly to perceptions of risk. I noted earlier the watchfulness and caution that seemed to permeate parents' practices when their children were in public view. Bruce described his own, as well as to his mind many other parents' "worst nightmare," which involved watching from the kitchen while children played outside, and the call to the authorities because they appeared to be unsupervised—exactly the experience of the Winnipeg mother.

Earlier, I noted Paula's experience of allowing her 4½-year-old to visit the park with a neighbour's children. In a world of watching eyes, it was a bold step. But a similarly bold step—having him play by himself in his own front yard—would be a step too far. Paula articulated the thinking of many parents on the subject of leaving children alone:

> I feel nervous when I pack the kids into the van and then I realize that I forgot my cellphone inside the house. And I have a momentary thought of, I can't leave the kids in the van while I run inside the house to get my cellphone. Of course I can, how ridiculous. I'm going to be two minutes. Honestly, they'd be fine in the van while I ran into the post office or anything as well. But you can't, because somebody will see.

Children's public exposure was always carefully monitored. Often the monitoring constrained what otherwise mature and responsible children were allowed to do. Penny, the mother of an independent nearly-5-year-year-old son, had her own memories of playing out on the street till dinner time. It wasn't something she would allow her son and his 10-year-old step-brother to do. "We live on a great street, don't get me wrong," she said. But times had changed. "Now you're worried about being judged."

Worries about being judged extended well beyond what external observers might see. I noted earlier the particular social and cultural context in which Canadian parents are raising their children, and the messages directed to them, from many sources, telling them what they should be doing. But, as many stories have also made clear, the transmission of these messages is not always benign. Parents feel judged by others, in the real and the virtual world, on how they are raising their children, how competent they are as parents. They feel guilt if they sense that they are not measuring up—though the measures in question may be unrealistic or unimportant. Gina, whose difficult start to parenting was described in the previous chapter, suggested another problem—the fact that struggles and hard times were not brought out in the open. "You don't talk about the struggles that you have," she said. "You judge your own self so harshly, because no-one ever talks about the hard part." Monica was a poignant case in point. She had decided to pick up her son from day care an hour or so later than she was technically able to, to give herself a break after work. "I felt very guilty about that, I felt terrible about that," she said. "I never even told anybody about that. I didn't even tell my husband actually." Aisha echoed her feelings. "As new moms, [we say] we're coping, and surviving, and everything is fine, but, it's not," she said. Aisha thought she might talk to her mother about some of the difficulties, but wouldn't confide in even her close friends. She belonged to an attachment parenting group, but knew personally only about two of the group's more than 600 members. "Online, it's easier [to be open], because you don't see each other," she said.

Among this group of parents, it was mothers rather than fathers who talked about expectations, judgment and guilt. "It's a universal thing," Karen said. Even as a home-based mother, able to devote more time to her daughter than if she were employed outside the home, she worried about whether she should be spending more time directly engaged with her, whether she was in enough activities, whether she had enough playmates. Fiona felt similar pressure:

It seems as though a lot of moms, and not even moms, just people around . . . can be judgmental about how you're bringing up your kids, and what you're doing. [It can be] really hard, especially if you're a new parent. Even me myself, looking at my friends, I'm guilty of that as well.

Suzanne, the free-play advocate introduced earlier, was dismissive of external judgment on her own account but could speak from professional experience on behalf of other parents who felt it keenly. Suzanne was a child-care consultant working with a provincial government agency. Her job was to offer support to parents coping with particular problems and children with special needs. She reported their fear of participating in groups with other parents because of the comments and questions they would need to parry—and the isolation that was often the consequence.

There were other sources of judgment. Leo, raising two children in a same-sex marriage, spoke frankly:

I feel we are under the microscope more so than straight families— only because, and I don't think it's a conscious thing, at least it's not in our circles, but I think that society, or maybe it's just in my head, I don't know, they almost want to see us fail, to prove that we are not fit to be parents, [that you] need a mother in a family in order to raise children. So I don't think I run my life with that notion in the back of my mind, but it's there.

Beth, with three young children, and in a privileged high-income dual earner household, felt the weight of societal expectations more specific to her situation. She framed them semi-jokingly as being about feeding kids organic food (in carefully prepared family meals), having them in many activities, and everyone being "well rounded." "It feels like it's too much," she said. "And everything seems to fall on women's shoulders." Beth felt she wasn't meeting those societal expectations. But after five years as a mother, she was less concerned about that. "I feel I meet my own expectations," she said, "because I've lowered the bar."

What Beth described as lowering the bar was reported by other mothers as learning from experience. Experience gave them confidence in the knowledge that they knew their own children better than anyone else. And that allowed them to tune out messages they perceived as critical and judgmental. "I think you can want to do everything the best that you can, and then get kind of bogged down with that," said Kate, the mother of five introduced in the previous chapter. "Sometimes you just have to be good enough." Jane, whose oldest child was 6, commented:

> I feel like I can trust my instincts. I feel like I have good kids. I also just feel like—I try to tell my friends [who have new babies, trying to do everything right], I just tell them, like, everyone is winging it. There's no [one] right way to do things. . . . Forget what other people are saying and just do what is working for your family.

As I noted earlier, mothers rather than fathers were the ones who talked about societal expectations, because mothers, in most cases, were the targets. Fathers were much less affected, and in some families could play an important role in reassuring mothers. Ben mentioned that his wife was currently stressed about a few child-related matters that weren't going as well as she'd hoped. That's was where he would come in. He would tell her:

> People have been doing this for thousands of years. Don't worry about it, you're going to be fine. . . . You're doing a great job, you're an amazing mother. You do what you do because you know what you're doing.

The fact that there is a *need* to allay worries, to tune out judgmental messages, to keep anonymous watchers always in mind, is significant. It points to a culture of parenting that is stressful at least to some degree for all parents. Against that backdrop, other concerns also emerged. Highly engaged fathers like Eliot and Kyle could not always find the kind of support in the community that seemed to be available to mothers. Chione, a recent immigrant from Egypt, was struggling to manage child-care in a cramped apartment while also studying for the exams she needed to pass to get Canadian certification in her medical field. The dual-earner households faced time constraints, that, when paired with the sleep deprivation that was sometimes also ongoing, often made daily life a struggle. Bruce commented: "There's never down time." Paula said, "I feel like everything in our lives revolves around trying to find little moments between our work schedules." That daily stress sometimes caused challenges in relationships. In Michelle's words, "The strongest relationships are put to the ultimate test, through new parenting." Five mothers mentioned depression as a current or recent concern. Annette had faced another category of life stress; in the year before we spoke, her husband had been treated for cancer.

There were sometimes challenges with individual children. Marie, employed full-time and the family's primary earner, had a 4½-year-old who was extremely anxious; he couldn't be left in his preschool group unless either his grandmother or his shift-working father stayed with him. Fiona, whose children were 4 and 2, wanted some strategies to deal with difficult behaviour. "There are just always hard times, when it comes to dealing with behaviours, or meltdowns," she said. "Those always challenge me . . . There can be some very tough moments . . .where you think [the effort] is not even worth it."

Fiona went on to add that there were good times too. But as Hélène pointed out, good times were hard won:

> I have an amazing partner, I have a great job with flexibility. My partner is a very involved father who takes on as much of the nurturing as I do, and it still feels like all the odds are stacked against us, in that the expectations of what we're supposed to be doing are not in line with the kind of supports that exist.

Hélène described the "almost project-like vibe" associated with raising children, the fact that outcomes were to be achieved even though parents weren't always sure what those outcomes were supposed to be. Moreover, added Hélène wryly, "we are supposed to have *power* over those outcomes."

Hélène's words are a neat summary of "parental determinism"—described in the introduction as the expectation that raising children is parents' sole responsibility. She also captured the sense of parenting, for this group, as being hard and rather lonely work. The happy situations where that wasn't the case stood out because they were unusual. Samantha, raising her twins in an exceptionally supportive community, was thoroughly enjoying her family life. But her comment about her situation was telling: "Parenting is great . . . but it requires the input of many, many people."

In conclusion . . .

In this chapter, I have tried to convey a sense of life on the ground for a particular group of parents of preschoolers. Our conversations focused on the big issues, but I also wanted to know what it was *like* for each of them, in their particular families, in homes and neighbourhoods across the country. Most parents in this group were well educated, and as far as I could tell, relatively privileged in the sense that their family lives were not beset by financial worries or other traumas. That made them, in most cases, well informed and thoughtful about what they were doing. And what they were doing was *parenting*. Parenting as a job, as work that was immensely rewarding, but also stressful and challenging, was very much the approach.

I have noted many of those "job" problems through the chapter—the sleep deprivation, the time pressures, the fairly widespread lack of support, the lack also of neighbourly sociability and a community interest in their children, all in a cultural context of surveillance and judgment. I am aware that this focus glosses the resourcefulness with which they handled many of the challenges, and their enjoyment of their growing children. But the challenges are worth noting. Most parents I spoke with still had a way to go before the intensity of preschooler child-rearing was over. They were still in the thick of it, and many were still fairly new parents. Their approaches—to children's learning, to issues of risk and independence, to their own needs as parents—would play forward in the years to come. How they responded to the challenges would make a difference.

6

Caring for older children

As the last chapter indicated, the preschool years can be gruelling for parents. Caring for children in those early years makes intensive demands, and parents alone are responsible, one way or another, for meeting them. Often they are managing without much support. So children's arrival at school age is an important turning point. In most cases, they are away from home now on a daily basis, and parents are able to shift responsibility for their daytime care to the school system. They are also past the "early years" developmental stage, with its relentless pressure on parents to optimize their brain potential, and make choices on a vast array of other issues. There is less bombardment of information. Children's shift to school may also allow a corresponding shift in the division of parental labour and the trajectories of care established in the preschool years. But while the (literally) hands-on child-care is now mostly over, some of the early parental dilemmas—about children's independence, and how they spend their time—remain lively. And as children grow, new questions and dilemmas emerge.

In this chapter, I introduce families in which most, if not all, the children were well launched at school. In 20 families, the preschool years were behind them—though there were differences in how far behind. Harry's 6-year-old was in school, and because they lived in Ontario, with full-day kindergarten, so was his 4-year-old. Beverley's children, aged 12 and 10, were at the other end of the age range. In 10 families, there was still a preschooler at home. But the experiences opened up to those parents by their older children are the ones I focus on here.

Configurations of family, divisions of labour, trajectories of care

In earlier chapters, I noted the difference that the presence or absence of siblings made to the experience of family life both for parents and children in the preschool years. Not surprisingly, that continued to be the case as children entered school (and some of the differences will become clear as this chapter unfolds). In this group, there were seven one-child families, and 13 families with two children. Eight families had three children (in one case a complicated co-parenting arrangement involving one father and two mothers). There was one family of four children. Finally, in Richard's family, introduced in an earlier chapter, children and step-children combined to make a family of five in another complicated co-parenting arrangement—and there was a new baby on the way.

In some of these families, as I suggested earlier, the divisions of labour established when children were younger did indeed shift when they were all in school. The most obvious shifts saw parents who had been home-based with preschoolers move into the workforce. In the seven families where couples were dividing the earning and caring work between them ("dual-dividers" like those introduced in an earlier chapter), four involved fathers who had previously been primary caregivers to younger children. Five other families were dividing earning and caring as co-parents in different households.

In four families, fathers continued to be primary caregivers, but only one included a dad at home full-time; in his case the issue may have been at least partly a lack of employment opportunities in his trades field. The three other fathers were all contributing to earning, in either part-time or full-time jobs, in families where mothers were in higher-paying professional careers. There were five dual-earner families in which mothers were taking on more of the family responsibilities. Two cases involved formerly home-based mothers moving back to paid employment when children were settled in school. In the case of Olivia and her partner, the sharing was between two mothers, with Olivia taking on the heavier caring load.

There were also six families with home-based mothers. Four of these families were part of the group with preschoolers still at home. But most of the home-based mothers were doing more than caring. Emma and Faye were completing university degrees part-time, with future career possibilities in mind. Rebecca, a former teacher and the mother of three children aged 12, 8, and 3, was home-schooling the two older children. Christine was a mother who formerly worked in a retail job while taking on most of the responsibility for two children. When we talked, the children were 7 and 2, and Christine was working full-time on a diploma in social work. The shifts, where they were happening, all seemed to involve parents looking forward and allowing more space to life outside parenthood.

The big decisions

I noted earlier the dilemmas for parents of older children that carried over from the preschool years—in particular, how children's time should be spent, and the amount of independence they should be allowed. When it came to time use, the big questions concerned children's involvement in structured, extracurricular activities, and also their access to screen time on the wide variety of electronic devices potentially available to them. Both areas had implications in terms of the amount of supervision perceived to be needed—and that, in turn, clearly linked to the degree of independence children were allowed. In our conversations, these were recurring themes.

Structured activities

In many families, children's entry to school meant a change, rather than a reduction, in the busyness. Nancy was the mother of two children, a son aged 6 and a daughter aged 4. Like Harry, she lived in Ontario, so her daughter had just started full-day kindergarten. I asked if life for her was now a little easier. "I don't know," she said.

> It feels like you just kind of move into these different phases, right? Now they're starting activities, so we have a very busy extracurricular activities schedule that takes over. Like once they're in bed and through the night, it's definitely night and day, better now, even though she still doesn't sleep through the night. But it's busy in a different way. You're not chasing them round the house, but you're driving here, there, and everywhere and watching them participate.

Nancy neatly summed up the day-to-day experiences of many of the parents I spoke with in this group. In fact, the topic of after-school activities came up in about two-thirds of the conversations, and in that group almost every child had some extracurricular experience. Some children were particularly active, and depending on how many children there were in a family, there were some highly scheduled parents too. Laura's nearly 7-year-old daughter Robyn was in after-school care; she also had speed skating, Beavers, and Taekwando during the week, and swimming on the weekend. Laura said she wondered if she was pushing the activities too much, but noted that a lot of the pressure to participate was coming from Robyn herself. Nancy's son was in hockey (with practices and games), and her daughter had cheerleading and skating. In the summer they both had swimming classes, and one other sporting activity. Most weeknights were taken up with the activity of one or the other child.

Max, with three daughters aged 9, 7, and 5, was probably the busiest of all the parents I spoke with. He was employed full-time, but was able to work from home; his flexible schedule positioned him as the primary care-giver—and chauffeur. All three girls had piano lessons and swimming. The 7-year-old was also in a gymnastics program that involved three 3-hour sessions per week. Co-ordinating their schedules saw Max and all three girls on the road after school on four of the five weekdays, and some of Sunday.

Children's enthusiasm was acknowledged to account for some of the busyness, and parents too wanted their children in certain activities. Valerie, employed full-time and the single mother of a 7-year-old and a 5-year old, thought music and swimming were important. But time was always at a premium. "It's hard to know what the right balance is," she said. "I mean, especially if kids *want* to do something." Tracy's 9-year-old was allowed two activities. Her parents picked piano and she picked gymnastics. Faye's three children, aged 8, 6, and 4, each had one—and only one—organized activity a week. Faye felt children needed to be bored occasionally. (When that happened, in her family, they tended to go outside and "build things" with their father.) Down time was recognized as important for older children too. At the other end of the age range, Ruth's boys, aged 15 and 11, were each allowed one activity a week, to allow time at home to decompress. Ruth reported that the night before she and I met, they had all played some board games. "You wouldn't have time to do that otherwise," she said.

The two families in which there were no extracurricular activities were those which included a baby, as well as school-age children—a fact that would have complicated scheduling for the home-based mothers involved. But the scheduling challenge was not the only reason. Julie firmly believed that her children needed unscheduled time. "Honestly, by the time they come home from school, they need to just play," she said. That playing, along with some reading, took up the space before dinner that organized activities might have occupied. Then it was time for bath and bed. "There's no time," she said. "I don't know how other people do it, but I know they do." Donna, whose husband had recently ended a period of unemployment, noted that extracurricular activities were too expensive.

The cost of children's activities was not mentioned by other parents. I have noted elsewhere that those I talked to were predominantly well educated, often in dual-earner households involving at least one professional job, so costs may simply not have been an issue. There was also not much talk about specific choices of activities, or the differences between sports and other physical activities, and those that were arts-based, and in many cases more expensive.[1] But children's widespread participation in extracurricular activities, and parents' belief in their importance, suggests another kind of pressure to conform that parents must accommodate or resist. Only Nadie, the Indigenous mother of an 8-year-old daughter, alluded to the dimensions of privilege that might accompany that pressure. Nadie's daughter wanted to learn ballet. In the dance studio in which she was enrolled, they were one of only three visible minority families. "You can see the class privilege," Nadie said. "Everyone dresses so well, and the kids, all their snacks are organic . . . . And the privilege—the way they talk to their dance instructors." Nadie herself was highly educated, and working in a professional job, but the dance studio was a challenge. "That's probably the only place I go now as an adult where I feel I don't fully belong," she said.

Screen time

For reasons that the foregoing may suggest, organized activities are not without their challenges. But what children are doing in their unstructured time may be even more challenging for parents, especially when those children are older. Screen time, an issue on the horizon for the parents of preschoolers introduced in the last chapter, was starting to loom large with this group of parents. In our conversations, they expressed many worries, linked at least partly to the ages of the children, and the sort of technology to which they had access. Parents worried about the educational content of streamed programs, about the cognitive effects of too much screen focus, about the social implications of time spent in a digital world, and for older children, about the content of websites, and the nature of cyber relationships. But there were also some striking differences between households in how these worries were addressed. Rules and limits took many different forms; what was considered appropriate in one family would be judged as far too permissive in another.

Max's children, whose busy after-school and weekend schedule was noted earlier, appeared to have the most screen access—and there seemed to be little differentiation between the oldest, at 9, and the youngest, at 5, in terms of their exposure. They spent a lot of time being driven to activities; Max noted that they would "fight like crazy" unless there was a movie playing on the screen in their van. At home, he said, they didn't watch TV, but instead were always watching YouTube videos, and discussing them together. They also made their own little videos, which they shared. And they were frequent Minecraft players. The 9-year-old had an iPad and was on FaceTime with her friends. Max was aware that this all amounted to a lot of screen time, and he often read Facebook posts debating the issue. But he didn't feel it was a concern for his own children. He noted that most of their screen time was interactive—and he saw that as preferable to hours of passive television watching. He did wish they were reading more. But he didn't see screen exposure as affecting their concentration span. "The one thing I worry about is the constantly needing to be entertained," he said. "But on the other hand, yeah, it doesn't bother me that much."

At the other end of the continuum, Harry's children, aged 6 and 4, had no screen time at all. The rule was that they could watch television when they were 7. When we spoke, Harry and his wife were limiting their own television viewing to the time when the children were in bed. Devices like iPads were not in the picture at all. Other parents of younger children were less restrictive, though there were rules about access in place. Isabel spoke of loading up a device with games for her 6-year-old when the family travelled. For Laura's nearly 7-year-old (whose busy extracurricular schedule was also noted earlier) there was no screen time before school, and perhaps 20 to 30 minutes twice a week after school. Other families spoke of relaxing limits on weekends, with Friday night movie nights featuring frequently. Terry, the father of a 7-year-old and a 5-year-old, was outspoken in his concern about digital technology. "I understand the importance of it," he said. "But we're raising a generation of zombies." His children were allowed to watch movies—but there were also "no technology" days, when the board games were brought out.

A common concern, at every age, and the reason the rules were needed in the first place, was children's apparent inability to monitor—and moderate—their own exposure to screens of any kind. Tracy's 9-year-old daughter Amy watched the YouTube videos Max's children enjoyed, along with music videos, and shows on television channels like YTV and Disney specially geared to pre-teens. "She would watch that all day if I let her," Tracy said. So the rule was under an hour of screen time a day, and only half an hour of that on the internet. Tracy had an app on her phone that allowed her to monitor what Amy was watching. "I think we are more vigilant than some of her friends' parents are," Tracy said. "Some of her friends definitely have more access to technology than Amy does. She has friends who have active phones, so they're texting. And we won't let Amy do that, to her chagrin." Yemi's oldest daughter was given a phone with no social media access when she was 12. This year, at 13, she was allowed some social media—but only with Yemi's approval. He said he didn't look over her shoulder, but instead gave her guidelines—and she knew he could easily access what she had been doing with the phone. Donna, the mother of three children aged nearly 10, 7½, and one, was at first delighted when their grandmother gave the older children iPads. But she soon noticed changes in the 7-year-old's behaviour when he had been on it too long. "He would just be really irritable and whine-y and cranky," Donna said. So she downloaded an app on her phone that allowed her to set specific times when the children had iPad access; when the time was up, the iPads shut off.

One inevitable outcome of parental monitoring of screen time was its withdrawal as a disciplinary measure. Several parents, including Donna, talked about screen time that would be lost as a consequence of children's misdemeanours. Debra and Cam, whose children were 11, 8, and 3, spoke of a confiscation in the year before we met that lasted three months—during which time the children "rediscovered toys." "The biggest challenge we have is the constant battle of balancing electronics," Cam said. Debra called it "a huge everyday battle."

Not all parents were willing to monitor so deliberately. Olivia, the mother of another 9-year-old, was reluctant to impose limits because she wanted her daughter to learn to impose her own, especially as, like Donna, she had noticed that too much screen time changed her daughter's behaviour. "We struggle with that," she said. So did Louise, the mother of 11-year-old Holly and 8-year-old Jason. "My kids know how to hang out without something in their hands," she said. "My big dilemma is how to get them to self-moderate. That's the thing I haven't figured out. Because they don't ever turn it [off] on their own." Instead, their mother had to tell them—multiple times, with shouting occasionally involved. "And I don't like that. Very soon, Holly is not going to be within my reach. . . . She needs to know how to put those things down."

Geoff, a single father co-parenting children aged 14 and 11, could tell her what the out-of-reach experience might be like. Though there was some family hanging out when the boys were with him, he noted that his older son would spend time in his room on his laptop. Geoff said he didn't know what that might involve. The older son also had a cell phone, which was intended mainly to allow his parents to be in touch with him. But Geoff said he mainly used it to visit websites. He was not good at returning his parents' calls or texts.

Ruth's experience with older children was different. Her sons, at 15 and 11, were at the stage of using the internet for legitimate school-based research. Ruth thought that electronic blocking of content didn't make sense, since in many cases it was the innocuous searches that could lead to inappropriate material. "Education is probably the best defence," Ruth said. So the boys were encouraged to talk about what they found online that made them uncomfortable—and they did. Modelling a practice at their younger son's school, they got him to talk about his "video of the day"—the one he had most enjoyed. Teaching him the distinction between content that made him feel good, and content that made him feel "creepy," was important. Ruth thought there was no point in fighting children's access to the internet; rather, it was important to discuss "cool sites," and what they enjoyed. "I think it's a healthy anxiety for parents to have, because we should be on top of it," she said.

Independence

Screen time for many older children was a digital time-out, a critical component of their unstructured time at home. It involved engagement with a world their parents couldn't readily enter, and didn't always understand.

For that reason alone, it might also offer a taste of freedom from parental supervision. As the discussion of screen time monitoring suggests, it was a world they were often disinclined to leave. Olivia, who noted earlier her reluctance to impose screen time limits, said of her 9-year-old, "Given the choice she would never leave the house."

Leaving the house—and leaving it unaccompanied by a parent—takes the discussion of children's independence to a different level. Whatever the cognitive or social risks of overexposure to the digital world (and I don't mean to dismiss them), children on their iPads in the family living room are physically safe, and sheltered from outside scrutiny. The real world poses risks of an entirely different kind. The parents I spoke with were acutely aware of them, but how they dealt with them depended on many factors.

The first linked to differences among parents themselves, in their sense of the importance of cultivating their children's independence, and their perception of the risks that independence might entail. Gail, the mother of 9½-year-old Curtis, was matter-of-fact about sending him to the park by himself. Louise, the mother of 11-year-old Holly and 8-year-old Jason, introduced earlier, was more thoughtful, but just as intentional about encouraging independence. "It's an ongoing conversation in our house," she said. "I'm very much like 'Go! Go fly! Go play!'" Louise's husband was not quite so adventurous, but she was working on his caution as the children demonstrated their competence and confidence. This was a biking family, and outside of the winter months, Louise biked to school with them. But Holly came home alone, and was happy to spend time at home alone if her mother and brother had activities after school. Both children were allowed to go to the nearby park, three blocks away, if they went with one another, or with a friend. The next stage of the conversation between Louise and her husband was about transport to school in the coming winter. Louise wanted them to take the city bus. "I think they're totally ready," she said. "They're both great kids, and super-responsible." Harry's children, at 6 and 4, were not at that stage. But Harry was training them for the sort of independence Louise's children were achieving. Part of the training was to spend a lot of time outdoors. The children's school had a huge grassy area, with big trees, where they loved to spend time every day. Harry said that sometimes they played with him, and sometimes they played with other kids, and sometimes the play lasted an hour and a half. Harry and his wife also used the park to work out, while the children played by themselves on the play equipment nearby. The family also went camping in the summer. Harry was a follower of US "free range kids" advocate Lenore Skenazy, introduced in Chapter 1. "It scares the stuffing out of me," he said. "I think that's part of being a parent." But he was also "a big believer." It was an approach he wanted for his children.

Alan, the father of two children aged 9 and nearly 6, could hardly have been more of a contrast. Asked about the extent to which his children were free to play and explore by themselves, Alan started his answer with a description of the family's strategies (using garage sales and the website Kijiji) to fill the house with toys, and—thanks to the "unfortunate reality of the time we live in"—organize play dates for the children. Alan conceded that it was "kind of not supervised play, but it kind of is." But, he said, "I can't do the alternate." Alan told a story that brought together many threads of parental decision-making about children's time use:

> We were at a park one time—at a friend's house, and they back on to a green space, and there was a park a little bit further down. And I couldn't even enjoy our conversation, even though I had a clear line of sight. All I could think of was, if some white van pulls up, I can't run over there fast enough. So what a horrible way to raise a kid. But I guess you compensate by giving them activities, getting them out there, giving them opportunities to meet other children, to make friends outside of school.

Henri, father of a 10-year-old and a 7-year-old, shared the philosophical commitment to children's independence that Louise and Harry described—and Alan's caution when it came to putting it into practice. "We do not walk our talk at all," he said. Henri's 10-year-old, whom his dad described as a very active boy, had been pushing to walk or bike to school. "And we have been petrified," Henri said. "Not because we're in a bad neighbourhood . . . The one road has crosswalk guards. There's really, rationally, there's not a lot of reasons [not to let him]." But Henri and his wife were both "scared to death—and it's ridiculous." Henri pointed out that, on the other hand, he was prepared to do things with his children that other parents might consider "borderline reckless." Both children had learned how to use an axe. They built things with him in the garage, and knew how to use saws and nail guns. The difference, clearly, was that Henri was present in the garage; he would not be present on an unaccompanied walk to school. But his son was challenging him, and he thought that perhaps the time had come . . . .

The second factor in shaping parents' decisions about children's independence, suggested already in the foregoing discussion, concerned the children themselves—what they were like, and how many of them were around. Henri's 10-year-old, itching for the independence of a solo ride to school, was like Laura's 6-year-old Robyn, introduced earlier. Laura spoke of her tendency to hover, when for example Robyn went out to visit a friend a block away. Laura would watch on the sidewalk till Robyn arrived, with Robyn saying, "You don't have to watch!" Robyn's school was not local, so she had to be driven. When she was older, she would take a school bus. "She would bus now if we would let her," Laura said.

Children within the same family were different. In Max's busy family, introduced earlier, there was a dependent and somewhat clingy older child, and a fiercely independent 7-year-old middle child. One of her treats, on swimming nights during the week, was to play by herself on the play structure at the Y while Max coordinated the other girls' lessons. Tracy's and Wade's 9-year-old Amy, introduced earlier, was much more cautious. They lived six blocks from her school, and there were plans for her to walk this year with a friend. But then Amy balked. "She identified that she doesn't feel safe," Tracy said. "She has integrated the message of stranger danger quite strongly. . . . It's something that's taught in school, it's something that we've taught her, and she's a bit leery." Instead, she caught the school bus, and her father walked her the one block to the bus stop.

Amy was an only child, a factor that may also have played into her reluctance to venture out on her own. Children with siblings close in age seemed more ready to be independent, and often had more autonomy—at least partly because family dynamics would have diffused parental oversight, and given each child the playmate that solo children couldn't always call on. In some multi-child families, younger children sometimes had much more freedom than many older solo children had. Julie's older children, aged 7 and 5, had just started to ride their bikes around the block on their own. "As long as they're together, they can do that," she said. In Julie's view, kids needed rules, "but they don't need to be constantly supervised." From the summer when they were 10 and 8, Beverly's children spent an hour a day on their own in the neighbouring park. Donna's older children were nearly 10 and 7½. Equipped with walkie-talkies and an elaborate check-in routine, they too were starting to spend time on their own at the park. In all three families, the presence of the older sibling gave the younger child more freedom from parental supervision than might otherwise have been the case.

A third factor, suggested only by a couple of cases, but perhaps generalizable to other families, was parents' wish to keep children close—and children's wish to *be* close—in the limited time busy working families had available. Laura, whose independent daughter Robyn didn't want to be watched, had a demanding professional job. She suggested that a tendency to hover came partly from the fact that she didn't see much of Robyn, and the times they were together were precious. Nick, co-parenting a 6-year-old and having her with him only half the time, didn't want to give up any of that time to anyone else when she was younger, and now was living with the consequences—a child who always wanted his company.

Children and community

Children's physical independence was also critically connected to where they lived. Rebecca's three children, aged 12, 8, and 3, were growing up on a farm close by a town in southern Ontario. This physical setting gave them an independence, not to mention access to the outdoors, that most city children did not have. They played outside, and also spent time with their father, helping with chores. The 12-year-old could already drive the tractor. Rebecca had also been home-schooling the older children. "I think people's perception is that [home-schooling parents] are the helicopter parents because they're around all the time," Rebecca said. "But I think it's actually the opposite. A lot of us joke about our 'free-range' kids, because they are, they're doing their own thing." Rebecca was part of two local home-schooling networks. She noted the extensive programming available through those networks, and also through the regular school system, to provide activities for home-schooled children and to bring their parents together. In this case, the "communities of place" described in earlier chapters had definitely been replaced by communities of shared interests—and they were vibrant communities.

Debra and Cam, whose children at 11, 8, and 3 were almost the same age as Rebecca's, lived in a progressive urban neighbourhood in Calgary—a different physical setting from the one Rebecca's family inhabited, but one that offered some of the same advantages. They were part of an emerging "community of place," in which the neighbourhood school was an important hub. The two older children walked to school by themselves, and knew a family on every block. Felix, the 11-year-old, was now allowed to explore the neighbourhood on his bike with his friends. The neighbourhood itself bordered a bluff near the river, set aside as undeveloped park land. All three children, along with others at the neighbourhood school, were frequent registrants in programs offered by the forest school located in the park. That was where Felix learned to whittle with a jack-knife and start a fire; he also got to try out a river raft. "All the parents that at least we know, we refer to [the neighbourhood] as the . . . bubble," Debra said. "It's a pretty unique neighbourhood within the Calgary community, I think. And so, what we view as acceptable and the norm might not be, beyond our bubble." The neighbourhood allowed Debra and Cam to give their children a taste of the freedom they themselves had enjoyed as children. "I would say our kids don't have a sense that they live in a large city," Debra said. "It's almost like a village."

Most of the families in this group lived in residential neighbourhoods in big cities, and the characteristics of the neighbourhood shaped the kind of physical independence children were allowed. Julie's boys could ride their bikes around the block because they lived in another Calgary neighbourhood, this time a quiet suburban one, with young families living nearby. The children in those families hadn't yet joined Julie's boys outside on their bikes, but Julie thought they probably soon would, since they now had a model to follow. Louise, introduced earlier, was willing to give her children the freedom they enjoyed at least partly because they lived on a pedestrians-only street in a vibrant, multi-cultural Montreal neighbourhood with many families. Olivia and her partner and 9-year-old daughter lived in Ottawa, in a little court of 42 houses, in which there were 23 children ranging in age from newborn to 12. Olivia spoke of the considerable interconnection between families that this physical setting made possible.

Isabel and her husband and their 6-year-old daughter Katie had recently moved to a house with a backyard, in a well-established neighbourhood in a rural Alberta town. Isabel hoped that this new environment would allow her daughter more freedom than she'd had in the past. It would be a learning experience for both Isabel and Katie. "I'm really nervous about it," she said. "And I don't know if it's because of the day and age that we live in, or general parenting anxiety, or the fact that so far, for her upbringing I haven't had the opportunity to give her a lot of that leeway." There was a community mailbox at the end of the street. Soon Katie would be sent to get the mail . . .

Pamela was co-parenting her 10-year-old son Tim in co-op housing in Vancouver, where they had lived since Tim was 3. Pamela described the co-op as "a little microcosm of a community within a big city." The co-op took up about half a city block, with green space and trees, and backed on to a park. There were a couple of other children Tim's age, whose range of play outdoors was allowed to expand as they got older. Pamela said that now they had some "free-range" play days outside. "I just have a special 'hoo-hoo!' that I do out the back door, to get them to check in," she said. "They'll go hours out there, running around." Pamela was aware, though, that the co-op environment was also sheltering Tim from exposure to the world outside. One day a few months before we talked, she had urged Tim to try walking from his grandmother's house, four blocks from home, across a busy street. With his mother watching from a little distance, he pressed the button to stop traffic at the crosswalk—but was too afraid to cross when the cars stopped for him.

Tim was, in his mother's words, "such a safe, cautious child." But his fear of traffic was a reflection of the fears of many parents, and limited the roaming range even older children were allowed. Ruth's boys, at 15 and 11 among the oldest in this group, obviously had more independence than younger children. From when he was about 12, the older boy walked to and from his neighbourhood school. Both boys, at 10, were given the freedom to ride their bikes in the neighbourhood, and shoot hoops in the school yard. But the current geographic boundary for the 11-year-old was between main streets.

Neighbourhood traffic was a concern because of the danger to unsupervised children it was assumed to be. But cars also worked to keep people separate, and isolated from their neighbours in environments where people seldom walked, or indeed were seldom outside their homes. Another less tangible concern, and a familiar one to the parents introduced in the last chapter too, was the extent to which people actually knew their neighbours. In some of the examples I've already provided, that community sense was there, and it made a big difference to what children were able to do—especially if the neighbours included families with other children. In other cases, neighbourhood sociability was in short supply. Faye, returning to Canada with her husband and three children after six years in Hong Kong, was struck by its absence in her residential neighbourhood. Here, she said, people drove their cars into attached garages, and shopped in big faceless grocery stores. Getting to know the neighbours took work.

She achieved it, almost inadvertently, by digging up the lawn in her front yard and establishing a garden one summer. She and the children were outside a lot; by being visible, and available for a chat, she made contact with neighbours she would probably not otherwise have seen, and the neighbours, ranging from older people to couples with babies, also got to know the children.

As Faye discovered, getting to know the neighbours could take work that not everyone would be prepared to do. Terry was another remarkable exception. The father of a 7-year-old and a 5-year-old, he described himself as "not only a provider, but a protector." It was as a protector that he wanted to know his neighbours. One strategy was the personal delivery of tins of Christmas cookies to people up and down their street. The children were allowed to ride their bikes as far as a certain bush—and Terry's door-to-door encounters ensured they knew every one of the neighbours whose homes they would pass. Terry would also consider letting the children go to the neighbourhood park, but first, he said, he would introduce himself at every one of the 27 houses along the way. "You have to know your neighbours, and to trust them," he said.

Terry's range of neighbourhood acquaintance was extensive, and his children were too young to be going too far afield on their own in any case. But even Terry would not be able to guarantee that the watchful eyes were always going to be friendly. Neighbours could also judge. Emma, the mother of a 9-year-old and a 6-year-old, had neighbours who were much more protective than she was inclined to be. "My biggest concerns are from my neighbours, not from my kids' safety," she said. In spite of her efforts at neighbourly sociability, Faye too conceded that she was more concerned about what the neighbours would think than what her children were capable of doing. And watchful eyes in the world outside the immediate neighbourhood were the same concern to most parents in this group that they had been to the parents introduced in the previous chapter.

To a great extent, parents took the likelihood of external judgment into account, and made sure that there was nothing in their public parenting practices to censure. But it was constraining; in this group too, it was hard not to be struck by the caution most parents demonstrated, when it came to allowing children time outside. In some cases the possibility of external judgment was even more constraining. Olivia, raising her 9-year-old in a same-sex relationship, said she and her partner were aware that if anyone reported them for some parenting fault, they might have to deal with homophobia in the system calling them to account. Nadie, the Indigenous mother, was aware of the racism that inflected how she was likely to be perceived.

Other parents, perhaps more secure in their social privilege, were prepared to offer some resistance. For example Julie said she was the parent who left her children in the car outside the bakery while she ran in for a quick purchase. She did it, she said "because I think there's not really a good reason why I can't do that. . . . If anything it's way more safe to leave them in the car than to take three children through the parking lot." Max agreed. And he "hated the culture" which suggested that such an action constituted parental negligence. "It's suffocating," he said. "You really do feel you've got to be hovering more than I would like."

At its most anonymous, what parents experienced was, in Faye's words, "surveillance with no community." But surveillance could also come down to judgment that was personal, and much closer to home. There were comments from this group of parents too about feelings of guilt—especially on the part of mothers—and the sense that, in Emma's words, "if something were to happen, especially the mother would get double blame." Nancy, the mother of two children introduced earlier, commented:

> I find it very difficult, because if you're at the park, and your child is doing something that maybe the other children wouldn't be allowed to do, then you feel like you're being judged, because you're not prohibiting them from climbing too high, or whatever it is.

Nancy was a community health nurse, with professional training in the developmental advantages of so-called "risky play." "There's good evidence backing it up," she said. "It's just . . . if yours is the only child out doing it." I asked Nancy if she talked about these kinds of situations with other parents—perhaps the parents of her children's friends. "We do," she said. "But we mostly talk about it in terms of 'Can you believe such and such is allowed to ride his bike through [street name], and his parents [aren't concerned]?'" Nancy was well aware that conversations like these contributed to the atmosphere of judgment—and risk aversion—that in another sense she would like to avoid. But in the circles in which she moved, those were the conversations. Ruth would have understood Nancy's dilemma:

> There is a big "What would people think?" And that's where, you've got to find your people, you've got to find people who think the same way, and have the same level of willingness to assess risk and say,

well, this risk is worth taking. . . . There's people who would probably take more risks than I would, and some who take a lot less. . . . You have to find your people, and you have to get to a place where you don't judge.

Finding support

"Finding your people," in the sense Ruth meant it, suggests the need for moral support for particular approaches to raising children. Parents of older children reported helpful online connections similar to those noted by the parents of preschool children, to help them find it. Pamela belonged to a co-parenting group on Facebook. Julie belonged to an online attachment parenting group. Other kinds of networks also formed. As noted earlier, Rebecca, home-schooling her two older children, was involved in two thriving home-schooling organizations near her southern Ontario home. "There's hundreds and hundreds of families doing it," she said.

There were other references to online research, or virtual contact with distant friends and family. But in this group of parents, information-gathering and the stress of trying to figure out what to do seemed to have diminished as the children got older. As the mother of the oldest children in this group, Ruth could take the longer view. "I definitely research," Ruth said. "If I've had an issue with anything I will google it. But in the past I think I was looking for a template for how to do everything, or like a perfect answer. . . ." Ruth's sense was that when children were under 5, parents believed they could control things. But as those children grew, they became their own people. The likelihood of full parental control moved from slim to nil.

Ruth's long view extended to the issue of hands-on, practical support as well. She commented that this kind of support was most needed when children were at the toddler stage—and at that stage in her own children's lives, Ruth said she didn't know how to ask for it. "I let myself get very isolated for a while," she said. A transition in Ruth's family occurred when her children reached school age, and their grandparents, not always around in the early days, became increasingly—and helpfully—involved.

Isolation had never been a problem for Nadie, the Indigenous mother of an 8-year-old and a 2-year-old, introduced earlier. Though the world outside her family might not always have been benign, family life was a different matter. There were family members on her First Nations reserve, and also a few doors down from her home in Calgary. She spoke of the support they provided on an ongoing basis. But it was support she also reciprocated, as part of a web of mutual obligation and caring deeply woven into her understanding of family. Nadie said her non-Indigenous husband sometimes struggled to understand the sharing of responsibilities and resources that came so naturally to her, but that also made individual decision-making more of a challenge. "I don't know what it's like to be alone," she said.

About half the parents in this group, like those introduced in the previous chapter, could count on support from family members—usually grandparents—close at hand. In many cases the support started early, and was ongoing. Beverly's parents provided child-care one evening a week when her first child, now 12, was 18 months old. That extended to a weekly overnight visit with two children, a routine that was still in place when Beverly and I met. The children were picked up after school on the sleepover day, and dropped off at school the next morning. Pamela, single and on a low income, had a mother who was willing to pool resources with her so they could jointly rent a more comfortable home. When he was younger, this grandmother also offered lots of child-care for Pamela's son. Nick, co-parenting as a single dad without family of his own around, was grateful for the support of surrogate grandparents who stepped in when he began a new relationship with their daughter.

I noted that the parents of preschoolers introduced in the previous chapter were less likely to call on friends for practical support, and this was the case with some of these parents too. "It's a funny thing," Louise commented. "I have a great group of friends with kids at about our age . . . I always thought there would be a lot more exchange of babysitting among my friends, and it doesn't happen that much." Help from friends took the form of emergency pick-ups from the after-school care program, but Louise noted also the time it took to arrange that sort of co-operation among working parents. It was, she said, "another level of management in the day-to-day."

Louise had the advantage, though, of being able to call on grandparents, who lived nearby and were always willing to help out. In the absence of family support, friends were sometimes much more involved. Julie, with three children aged 7, 5, and 6 months, made local friends from her online attachment parenting group. "That's kind of where I met *everybody*," she said. "And that's still where I go." Julie couldn't call on family help, but said she would call on friends "without a doubt" if she had to. In two other cases neighbours became the friends who stepped in to provide help. Emma, the mother of two children aged 9 and 6, recalled the early years with her first child as isolating to the point where she felt suicidal. But when her second child arrived, she was resourceful about finding help. Among other connections at that time, she was part of a neighbourhood babysitting co-op. Olivia, similarly isolated when her now-9-year-old was younger, also had neighbours now as a source of support. As noted earlier, Olivia and her partner lived in a court of houses with 22 other children, aged newborn to 12. "So we've all kind of helped each other out and raised each other's kids, so that has been really really valuable," she said. "It's probably been our main support." Faye, the mother of three children now aged 8, 6, and 4, had lived in Hong Kong following her husband's job transfer. Their first child was then 2 months old, and Faye knew nobody. But she got to know a handful of women whose partners had been transferred at the same time. All were mothers, living close at hand, and none was in paid employment. They had the resources, in a vibrant city well set up for expatriates, to help each other.

With older children, the help that was needed was more logistical—the sort of after-school pick-ups Louise mentioned (however challenging they might be to organize), the carpooling to extracurricular classes, and supervision on days when schools were closed. This was the context in which parents got to know the parents of their children's friends. Beverly's children were competitive swimmers. Asked about support from friends, she commented that it was mostly now the "swimming parents" she sat with at the pool a couple of times a week. Tracy spoke of texting back and forth with parents of their daughter's friends, on practical matters. "And we do compare notes a little bit, like 'What time are you doing bedtime?' . . . 'I heard this from her, what did you hear?'" Tracy said. "So we're doing a little bit of that kind of thing."

But isolation was an undercurrent in many other accounts. Cora, a single immigrant mother from Sudan with children aged 12, 8, and 5, depended on a church community and a local family support agency. There were few friends. Faye, whose friendships in Hong Kong were such a resource, spoke of the shock of returning to Calgary, where that easy neighbourly sociability was missing. "It's so isolated here," she said. Laura commented that her husband, an extroverted stay-at-home caregiver when their daughter was a preschooler, had been active in creating networks of friends in the community. As the employed parent, in a demanding professional job, she had online connections with distant family and friends. But she didn't have the time to make the local connections her husband was so good at, and she was rather lonely. Valerie, as a single mother of a 7-year-old and a 5-year-old, was even more time-stressed, and lonely too. "It's hard to *have* any friends," she said.

Among these parents there were also some lonely fathers. It was hard not to notice that the opportunity I gave them to talk about their children, and themselves as fathers, was a rare experience for several. I asked Wade whether he had people he could call on to talk to. "Hmmm," he said. "Well, to be honest, it's sometimes difficult for me to cultivate those supportive relationships. I sometimes just don't put the time in . . ." Kofi, thinking back to his oldest child's early years, when he was co-parenting as a single father, said he would have asked for help, but "I just felt there was no-one to ask." Yemi, an immigrant from Nigeria with four children, said that he sometimes felt that he was on his own, and wished he had family to visit. (On the strength of our conversation, he thought he would try to connect with some other parents.) Richard was now in a much happier family setting. But he had been a single parent for several years, and recalled the feeling of isolation as "the hardest part of all." He had joined a fathers' network run through a non-profit family support organization in his community to give himself people to talk to . . .

(More) challenges and concerns

At the end of many of my conversations with parents, I asked about "things that were on their minds." Tracy, the mother of 9-year-old Amy, said:

> It does sadden me, that she doesn't get a lot of just down time. I sometimes wonder if she gets enough just being a kid time. Because we pick her up from after [school] care, we come home, we have supper, if it's an activity night we're out the door. We do homework. She gets maybe half an hour and then we walk the dogs and we're off to bed. So I do worry, it saddens me that she doesn't get more just down time. So we try to fit that in in other ways . . . but it's a fitting in rather than the norm.

Tracy's description of a typical day, and her feelings about it, would have resonated with a great many of the parents in this group. Almost all of them were very busy, and so were their children. There was a lot of driving—to and from work, to and from school and after-school care programs, to and from scheduled activities. And the busyness had some possibly unintended consequences, apart from the lack of down time.

The first—no surprise, given the earlier discussion of children's independence—was that many children had very little time away from adult supervision of one kind or another. As also noted earlier, they (therefore) didn't always seek it—and some parents found reasons not to provide it.

A second consequence, also unintended but significant, was that many children seemed to spend very little time outdoors. There were notable exceptions, some of them mentioned earlier—children like Harry's urged to play outside, and children like Debra's and Cam's registered in forest schools. The after-school program in which Valerie's daughters were registered was in a forested area, and the girls were outside almost all the time they were there. Gail, whose university degree was in kinesiology, was adamant about ensuring her 9-year-old son got the requisite 60 minutes of outdoor activity a day. He was also taken on hikes and canoe trips, and went camping. Even Alan, whose extreme caution was noted earlier, took his children camping. But my sense from many conversations, and the structure of many family days that I heard about, was that time outdoors was at a premium. Rebecca's children, growing up on a farm, were outside much of the time. But as a former elementary school teacher, she raised the issue of the "nature deficit" described in the introduction, as a possible concern for many city children.

The third consequence related specifically to parents. It linked to a comment made by Louise, whose determination to encourage her children's independence was noted earlier. Louise spoke of the social expectation that "parents should be sort of omnipresent in their children's lives." Louise thought she was countering this expectation with her own children. But the organization of days like Tracy described, commonplace in many families with school-age children, would almost guarantee parental omnipresence, whether or not the parents themselves wanted it.

Many parents did. Max, the very busy chauffeuring father introduced earlier, said:

> For me it's great. I love being a dad. I love to drive my kids around, be with my kids doing their activities. . . . If anything, I wish I was spending more time volunteering at my kids' school, and took more

of those days off. . . . More and more, I'm growing into enjoying all the parenting.

But it was also not hard to see how little time would be left, in his household and many others, for anything else. Parental omnipresence can have the further effect of creating families that are intensely child-centred. Parents, as well as children, have limited independence as a consequence.

In some cases, the challenges of child-rearing were compounded by health and other concerns about individual children. Tracy's and Wade's daughter Amy had Type 1 diabetes. That diagnosis, they thought, had compounded her existing caution and reluctance to be on her own. Beverly's children had celiac disease; her encouragement of their independence had to be accompanied by the stringent policing of any activities involving food. Terry and his wife had recently been shocked to learn that their 7-year-old son, who had been in trouble at school for some time, had serious vision and hearing loss, among other health concerns. And these were not the only cases.

Parents sometimes had problems of their own. Co-parenting relationships were occasionally stressful, when there was disagreement on child-rearing issues. In Gail's case, co-parenting was allowing her to move by herself to another city to undertake a special university program. She spoke highly of her former partner, who was holding the fort at home during term time. But she desperately missed her son. In another sad conversation, a father spoke of leaving his marriage because he was gay. He had joined a gay fathers' group, but didn't plan to come out to his children for the foreseeable future. For the moment, he said, he was telling himself it didn't matter. He was not worried about their emotional wellbeing. "I think I do pretty well there," he said. "I'm more worried about my own emotional wellbeing."

It's important not to overstate the problems. Even when they loomed large, they didn't overwhelm parents' joy in *being* parents. Julie was one of the most contented mothers in this group. I asked her what had been the best part of being a parent. "I don't think there is one best part. It's all been really lovely," she said. "I would say it's 90 percent good, 10 percent hard. . . . And then the hard stuff is almost always worth it." Isabel would probably have put the "hard stuff" at higher than 10 percent. And she noted that it was "really easy, day to day to get locked in to that a bit," especially when dissenting voices, online and elsewhere, challenged her confidence. But a friend's posted message—"comparison is the thief of joy"—had resonated with her. "I think I should in some ways just get on with it . . . and maybe not sweat it so much," she said.

In conclusion . . .

In this chapter, I have tried to capture some of the key issues confronting parents when their children reached school age. I wanted to explore the differences in family life that might emerge when children got older, and were less dependent on hands-on parental care.

There certainly were differences. Kids' time in school freed some parents to resume employment. In some cases children took up activities that parents themselves had enjoyed. There was the pleasure of seeing children develop their own skills and interests, and in supporting the people they were, and were becoming. Parents were also following, not always happily, their children's growing participation in the digital world.

But some things did not change. Parents continued to be very busy, and their children were busy too. There was very little down time, for anyone. Parents also continued to be very much the bearers of responsibility for their children, even though school was now in the picture. They were subjected to the same external scrutiny and judgment that the parents of preschool children also reported. And for that reason, many found it hard to let go, even in situations where children were quite capable of managing on their own, and even when parents remembered—as many did—how different their own growing up had been.

The requirement of parental omnipresence noted earlier was not new to them. It had begun for most parents in the preschool years. But it seemed to be an ongoing requirement as children got older. It was the product of an environment of surveillance and judgment that was seldom challenged, and hard to resist. It was an environment that *trained* parents to be omnipresent—and virtually ensured that raising older children would be challenging and sometimes lonely work too.

PART III

Looking Forward

Looking forward is a deliberate play on words. I use it in the sense, first, of a look at what might lie ahead, for parents of young children in Canada. But I also mean it in the sense of hopeful anticipation of positive change— change that might be slow in coming, but that is change for all that.

Looking forward, in both senses, needs to be grounded in a realistic view of the present, and that's the ground I cover in Chapter 7. Even for someone who tends to see cups that are half full, it is not a cheerful picture. While wanting to avoid nostalgic comparisons with my own child-rearing experiences three decades ago, it was hard not to be concerned about many of the big differences I saw—the bombardment of information, the frequent social isolation, the fear of external judgment and surveillance, among others.

What is shared, by parents of every generation, is concern for children. What parents do is always guided by what they think children need. So Chapter 8 takes a much closer look at children, and at new ways of thinking about what they need—ways that might be much better for them, and which might liberate their parents from the burden of mostly unreasonable expectations many of them are facing. There is also discussion of some initiatives at the policy, community and individual level that parents might find helpful.

7

The story so far

I began this project as an exploration of contemporary "parenting culture" in Canada, on the assumption that things had changed considerably for parents in the decades since I was raising young children. After some two years of background research, and, more recently, many months of talking with parents, I have had my assumption resoundingly confirmed.

There has been change in almost every dimension of child-rearing— starting at the most visible and basic level, with all the equipment. I think back more than three decades to my son's grandparents, commenting with interest on his feeding gear. Items like sippy cups and bowls with suction bases were standard items by then, but not in their day. And I wonder what many of today's grandparents would make of bassinets, complete with recorded lullabies, soothing vibrations, and a nightlight, set up to swivel over the parents' bed, or the video monitors that are now also standard equipment. Today's grandparents, raising children in the days before the internet and social media, would perhaps be even more bemused by the phone app with on-the-spot suggestions for averting a toddler's tantrum,[1] or the one offering a detailed "milestones checklist" for children up to 5 years of age.[2]

I too was bemused by some of the changes, and delighted by others (balance bikes for preschoolers come to mind). But many of the less tangible changes gave me pause. More than anything I was struck by how *hard* the work of raising kids now seems. I came to this conclusion again and again in the course of my conversations with parents. Many months ago, on the recommendation of one mother, I read the popular parenting book *Why Have Kids?*, by US author Jessica Valenti.[3] Recently, looking back over my notes on the book, I found I had written: "In a nutshell, it makes the point that raising children is unbelievably hard work that no-one tells you about, and it's unlikely to make you happier on a daily basis!" This message had clearly resonated with the mother who recommended the book, and with legions of other parents as well, if its popularity is anything to go by.

US journalist Jennifer Senior's description of contemporary parenthood as "all joy and no fun" would also have resonated with many of the parents I spoke with. Her perspective, described in the introduction, is worth revisiting here. She notes the difference between *being* a parent, and enjoying all the moment-to-moment pleasures of being in a relationship with a child, and *doing* "the quotidian and often arduous task of parenting." Senior considers that ever since *parenting* became a popular verb, "there has been an even greater emphasis on child-rearing as a high-performance, perfectible pursuit."[4] That emphasis, its links to new thinking about children and risk, and the extent to which parents now seem to be held accountable for every move they make, are issues I take up in what follows.

The problem with "parenting"

I have noted in earlier chapters the fact that *parenting*, as a job, was very much the approach that informed most of the messages, both formal and informal, directed to Canadian parents. That came through in my conversations with parents too. What I haven't mentioned so far though is the extent to which elements of this approach have been formally studied—and challenged. The problem is not just that, when it comes to raising children, no approach (to quote Senior again) can be "perfectible." It's rather that the heavy focus on the *doing* sets up parents' relationships with their children in ways that many researchers find troubling. A common concern is that *parenting* draws too heavily on the perspective and language of developmental psychology, with its focus on particular practices of parents leading to desirable outcomes in children. For example, it's the perspective that guides widely known parenting programs like Triple P, described in Chapter 1. There I noted the many levels of support and information in the Triple P structure, with core parenting skills specified even at the most basic level. (For example, skill areas included "parent-child relationship enhancement"—which involves, among other things, "spending brief quality time," "talking with children," and "showing children affection.")

The Triple P program has come in for considerable criticism, partly on the basis that its claims don't match the empirical evidence of its achievements.[5] But a criticism that can be applied to contemporary sources of parenting information more generally is the tenor of the advice. Injunctions to parents to talk with their children, or to show them affection, are like the advice I noted in the "Eyes on Parents" brochures also described in Chapter 1. (For example, "Show your child that he can trust you to be supportive and to take care of him when he needs food and comfort.") Sociologist Glenda Wall, in a recent study of materials used in an Ontario government-supported parenting program, describes a video segment geared to teach parents how to be sensitively attuned to their children. They are told: "Listen to your baby. Learn to follow your baby's cues. Watch your baby's posture, hand and eye movement. Is your baby alert? Or is your baby sleepy? . . ." Wall comments, "What is being suggested here would seem to be simple communication skills that involve paying attention to basic non-verbal cues, something that most adults would have long ago mastered."[6] Another critic observes that much contemporary "positive parenting" advice on discipline can be boiled down to "Be nice."[7]

Advice like this is only spelling out what parents would be doing anyway.[8] Another researcher[9] calls it "codifying the minutiae of parenting" in a way that transforms all these basic, everyday activities into tasks geared to specific outcomes. As researchers Stefan Ramaekers and Judith Suissa put it, parents

> no longer (just) live together with their children in a family, but "interact" with them; when parents buy toys for their children this is no longer (just) something one speaks about in terms of the concept of "playing," but in terms of creating stimulating environments for their children, and in terms of what this playing is good for (i.e. what particular capabilities it will develop); reading stories to one's children is something one speaks about in terms of opportunities for bonding and for stimulating children's linguistic capabilities, etc.[10]

It is a very instrumental approach, one that Ramaekers and Suissa call "a narrow and impoverished way of conceptualizing child-rearing and the parent-child relationship."[11] It discounts all the other aspects of the relationship that are also immensely valuable. Reading to a child undoubtedly "provides opportunities for bonding" and "stimulates the child's linguistic capabilities," but the same activity could be reframed as a lovely and familiar ritual that soothes both parent and child, and makes them happy. Bonding is a natural outcome, but to set out with that goal in mind distorts the whole undertaking. That's also the concern behind a shift in the way mothers' attachment to their babies is viewed. Where once it was seen as a concern only on the rare occasions when (usually for understandable reasons) it didn't happen, it has come to be viewed as a "task" all mothers must formally undertake.[12]

Other scholars raise other problems with the developmental psychology perspective. Martin Woodhead, a UK professor of childhood studies, argues that it homogenizes all forms of child development into the one most familiar to privileged middle-class parents, and also discounts children's own individuality and agency. Woodhead further contends that it inspires a way of thinking about children as "a set of 'potentials,'" as "becomings," rather than beings.[13] The end goal of this "becoming" is a particular kind of idealized adult. In this sense, as another scholar, Alison Gopnik, puts it, parents are acting like carpenters; they see their job as to shape the material they are working with into the final product they have in mind.[14] Gopnik is herself a developmental psychologist, but one who is deeply concerned about the "parenting" model of raising children.

A final concern, implicit in much of the foregoing, is that the "parenting" model puts the onus on parents, and parents alone, to master the skills needed to produce the required outcomes in their children. (This was defined in the introduction as *parental determinism*.) In this context a comment made by Hélène, one of the mothers introduced in Chapter 5, bears repeating. Hélène said:

> I have an amazing partner, I have a great job with flexibility. My partner is a very involved father who takes on as much of the nurturing as I do, and it still feels like all the odds are stacked against us, in that the expectations of what we're supposed to be doing are not in line with the kind of supports that exist.

Hélène didn't make the point explicitly, but in practice, as many researchers (and many of the parents I spoke to) point out, mothers are the primary targets—of both the advice, and the blame when things go wrong.[15]

Risk revisited

I noted in the introduction the connection between parental determinism and changing ideas about risk, particularly the *consciousness* of risk that shapes so much thinking about what children need, and what parents should be doing. The focus is on identifying potential problems, and then working to prevent their occurrence—however unlikely the occurrence might be. In Chapter 1, I described the universal, population-based approach of the Triple P parenting program, which, like other public health measures, is intended to "inoculate" families across the board against possible future concerns. That's the thinking too behind the advice to parents, also mentioned in Chapter 1, on "resilience" training for children—all children, not just those growing up in challenging circumstances. The implicit message, in all the advice and information, is that children's cognitive and emotional development may be at risk if parents don't toe the prescribed parenting line.

Risk consciousness also extends to children's physical safety. The dual perceptions of children as fragile and vulnerable, and the world (and the people in it) as full of potential dangers, combine to constrain the lives of parents and children in many ways. For children, as earlier chapters have mentioned, one of the casualties has been free outdoor play—the sort of play many of the parents I spoke with remembered from their own childhoods. Many Canadian scholars are now investigating the current "state of play" from the perspective both of children and their parents.[16]

A key researcher in this field, whose work is internationally known, is Mariana Brussoni, a developmental child psychologist at the University of British Columbia, whose lab at the BC Children's Hospital Research Institute[17] has produced multiple interdisciplinary research projects focusing on many aspects of play. The springboard for all the research is the recognition of the decline in children's play outdoors. Some studies have focused on parents' perceptions of risk in children's play.[18] Others have examined particular play environments;[19] in this context Brussoni and her colleagues have noted the generic, cookie-cutter nature of most playground equipment currently available in children's playgrounds, and their separation from the natural environment. A critical underpinning of the Brussoni approach is the understanding that keeping children as safe as possible—the current public health goal—is not necessarily in their best interests from a developmental standpoint.[20]

Concerns about traffic, and about "stranger danger," are common justifications for parental protectiveness; one place they appear is in research on children's geographic mobility in their neighbourhoods.[21] These concerns among others help account for the findings, in other studies, of the dramatic reduction in the scale of children's independent movement. One study[22] used GPS monitoring and other data sources to examine the movements of a sample of 9- to 13-year-olds from seven schools in an Ontario city. The researchers found that their participants spent more than 75 percent of their time outside school in an area very close to their homes—and most spent more than half of this time indoors at home. They noted that the "vast majority" of the children were subject to household rules that restricted their opportunities for independent travel outside, and which had the effect of limiting their activity to a very narrow range immediately around their homes. The parental restrictions were "a powerful influence."[23]

Parents' perceptions of unstructured play, and play outdoors, were the focus of a survey of more than 1,600 parents of children aged 5 to 12, conducted by the City of Calgary Parks and Recreation department in 2016.[24] While there was widespread support for both activities and the benefits they could provide for children, 90 percent of respondents could also provide reasons that got in the way of such play, or could suggest ways to make it more widespread. Lack of time was the major inhibitor, and fears about traffic, neighbourhood safety, and the absence of other children as playmates were also noted. "Community norms . . . there are no kids outside," one parent commented. "Mine is the only one that walks to school." Children's attitudes also drew comment. One parent observed, "I think they are too hooked on screens, their creativity is not great and games and technology offer more rewards in their brains." Another barrier parents perceived related to the surveillance and judgment described many times in earlier chapters. As one respondent put it: "Judgement by others—worry that neighbours will report unsupervised play to authorities and therefore scaring the kids."

These findings are in line with the comments of most of the parents I spoke with. Outdoor time for children seemed to be at a premium. While many contrasted their own relatively free-range childhoods with those of their children, there was widespread agreement that children today needed much more protection and supervision. Neighbourhood type and particular living arrangements clearly made a difference, as some of the parents pointed out in earlier chapters. Samantha's island community, Louise's pedestrians-only urban neighbourhood, and Pamela's co-op housing made it easier for each of them to relax their supervision, and these mitigating factors also showed up in the research.[25] But I noted in many conversations the parental watchfulness and caution that accompanied their descriptions of children's encounters with the world outside their homes. And though few were as concerned as Alan, introduced in Chapter 6, about stranger danger and child abduction, they worried about traffic, and they worried about the absence of other children in the spaces they might otherwise be willing to let their children play. Above all, though, they worried about the surveillance and judgment they were sure would follow the smallest lapse in vigilance. And as I also noted in earlier chapters, worries about being judged extended well beyond what external observers might see. Parents—mostly mothers—felt judged by others on their competence in raising their children. It seemed to me, after many conversations, that this atmosphere of surveillance and judgment was one of the biggest challenges contemporary parents had to face.

Surveillance and judgment

The sort of surveillance that resulted in trouble for that Winnipeg mother, whose children were reported as being unsupervised in a fenced backyard, continues to occur, and to get media attention. In September, 2017, for example, the British Columbia Ministry of Child and Family Development stepped in to prevent a Vancouver father from allowing four of his five children (aged 7, 8, 9, and 11) to take a city bus to and from school. The children had been carefully coached over several months, and were busing without any problem until an anonymous complaint ended the arrangement. The father was told that in BC children under 10 could not be left unsupervised "in the community, at home, or on transit," and that a child under 12 could not be responsible when no adult was present. The story garnered many comments, mostly supportive of the father, when it was published in the *Globe and Mail*.[26] According to the father, there was also considerable support on social media.

My sense is that the parents I talked with might think the BC father was pushing the limits of public tolerance with this initiative. But the incident would probably serve to strengthen their belief that watching eyes were everywhere. And while some, as I noted in Chapter 6, might be confident enough to challenge those watching eyes on occasion, many would agree with Max, who hated the "suffocating" culture that required parents to hover more than they might want.

In the introduction I described a study by US researchers[27] who investigated this phenomenon. In a series of online surveys using randomly distributed vignettes, they asked participants to gauge the risk to children of being left alone in a variety of circumstances. In every case, there was objectively little actual risk involved. What varied in the vignettes were the reasons given for why the children were left alone. As I noted, participants perceived the risks to be much greater when they thought the children had been left deliberately, rather than unintentionally. In other words, they were making *moral* judgments. The researchers commented that it wasn't just that people thought leaving children alone was dangerous and therefore immoral; they also thought it was immoral, and therefore dangerous. And they overestimated the actual danger to children in order to justify their moral condemnation. The researchers went on to say:

> Our findings suggest that once a moralized norm of "No child left alone" was generated, people began to feel morally outraged by parents who violated that norm. The need (or opportunity) to better support or justify this outrage then elevated people's estimates of the actual dangers faced by children. These elevated risk estimates, in turn, may have led to even stronger moral condemnation of parents and so on, in a self-reinforcing feedback loop.[28]

It's one way to account for the surveillance phenomenon. The prior question is how the norm came to be established in the first place. The researchers suggest it has something to do with what they call the *availability heuristic*, which proposes that the easier it is for a person to think of a bad thing happening, the more frequently they think it happens. Round-the-clock news coverage of events like child abduction, statistically rare though they are, makes bad things easy to recall. But as one of the researchers, Ashley Thomas, commented in a radio interview, it is worth noting that this norm has not arisen everywhere. "For example, I was in Norway earlier this year and people left buggies, strollers with infants outside of stores while they went inside to get coffee or have lunch with a friend," she said. "You never see this in the States." (She could have added that you would never see it in Canada either.[29]) Instead, we have what sociologist of childhood Ivar Frønes calls a "culture of fear (as well as risk)." [30]

We also have a culture of judgment and competition, as earlier chapters have frequently indicated. In many conversations, with mothers in particular, fear of being judged was described as shaping decisions and practices. It cast a shadow over the experience of being a parent. Judgment was perceived not only in personal encounters—playgrounds were common sites—but also through online and social media commentary. In the digital world in particular, models of "perfect" mothering abound. In Chapter 1 I noted researchers' concern with the practice of "sharenting"—the posting of pictures and information about children that often tended to (over)emphasize the positive at the expense of more realistic depictions of family life.[31] Mothers, understandably invested in the child-rearing choices they make, tend to become "tribalized," and there is a slide from what (mothering) practices might be best for baby, to who is the best mother. Researchers call this "performative mothering,"[32] and note one of its outcomes—the tendency of mothers to *participate* in the atmosphere of judging. Several mothers I spoke with acknowledged, ruefully, that they were occasionally part of the problem.

Resisting these tendencies takes work, and also a lot of confidence, as several of the mothers introduced in earlier chapters demonstrated. (I will have more to say about those mothers in the next chapter.) But other mothers struggled with social expectations they felt they were not meeting. Gina, whose difficulties with her first baby persuaded her not to have a second, said: "You judge your own self so harshly, because no-one ever talks about the hard part." Michelle attributed her unhappy early years with her son to her failure to match the "perfect" mothering she thought her friends were modelling.

Thinking back, Michelle wondered whether her difficulties might have been compounded by post-partum depression. She was not the only mother who spoke of it. In fact seven mothers said they had suffered at least to some extent from post-partum depression or anxiety in at least one of their pregnancies. Canadian statistics suggest that this is the case for some eight percent of mothers,[33] with a higher proportion experiencing post-partum anxiety.[34] While biological and possibly genetic factors are involved,[35] social factors have also been found to be critical, with some researchers suggesting that the failure to meet the "perfect mother" expectations (which include successful breastfeeding) may contribute to mothers' distress. Sociologist Stephanie Knaak conducted an intensive study of Canadian mothers whose post-partum emotional states ranged from mostly happy to clinically depressed. Having enough help was one common stress mitigator; so was having realistic beliefs and expectations. Knaak observed that a common thread in her interviews was how mothers' beliefs and ideas about what they "should" need, "should" be, and "should" do shaped their ability to activate the resources they needed.[36]

Coping in context

Child-rearing is challenging for all parents—but some face extra difficulties. A salutary reminder, on the subject of post-partum depression, comes from research suggesting immigrant women are at greater risk.[37] Many immigrant parents suffer the additional disadvantage of being very far from family support. Jessica, Ade, and Aisha, introduced in earlier chapters, all spoke of this. So did many of the parents interviewed by researchers documenting the effects of recent policy changes limiting the sponsorship of immigrant family members.[38] In many cases, grandparents provide crucial practical and emotional support to immigrant parents, who frequently need two household incomes to manage financially, and who can't afford the prohibitive cost of child-care.[39]

The research by sociologist Angele Alook[40] on Indigenous families is another reminder of the extra challenges some parents face. Alook's research focused on patterns of migration between her own traditional community in Wabasca, Alberta, and the city of Edmonton. She found that children's best interests dictated most of the moves, and also noted the importance of grandparents, in a broader context of Indigenous understandings of family relations. For Alook the centrality of the family, and of the child within the family, are understandings that have persisted despite, in her words, "the pathologization of Indigenous parents" over the long and traumatic history of colonialism in Canada. One of the mothers in her study spoke of leaving an abusive relationship and staying in a women's shelter, then returning to school, getting a stable job and finding long-term housing. "I was motivated for my son, not to go backwards," she said.

Other challenges cross cultural and other boundaries, as some of the parents introduced in early chapters made clear. Annette spoke of her husband's cancer diagnosis and treatment. Balancing children's needs with a parent's serious illness[41] introduces a whole new level of stress and worry. The challenges are compounded too for parents with disabilities,[42] and for parents like Terry, or Tracy and Wade, dealing with illness in their children. For same-sex parents like Leo and Mitch, external surveillance and judgment may be exacerbated by homophobia. Valerie and Clive were managing as single parents—and in Valerie's case also managing a difficult co-parenting arrangement with her children's father.

In Chapter 2 I introduced a variety of other circumstances that could be expected to shape the experience of family life across the board—circumstances like where people lived, the work they did, and the availability and quality of child-care. In my conversations with parents the significance of these three issues became abundantly—and sometimes painfully—clear. They too served to differentiate families. On the work front, I spoke to federal civil servants like Annette and Evan, in secure well-paying jobs with generous benefits, and to self-employed parents like Pamela and Kyle whose work was less secure, less well remunerated, and probably more stressful for those reasons. Their experiences echoed the findings of research I cited in Chapter 2, showing that the balance of work and family responsibilities was difficult even for the most privileged workers. Andrea's situation illuminated another work-related concern. She wasn't employed because no job for which she was qualified would pay her enough to cover child-care costs. Andrea lived in the Greater Toronto Area—a region where child-care costs are particularly high. But as I noted in Chapter 2, that's a problem to some extent across the country. Only in Quebec, as Montrealer Louise observed, was child-care cheap enough to make any mother's wish to return to work feasible.

Location mattered not only because of child-care costs, but also because of the availability of affordable housing. As Chapter 2, also noted, parents in cities like Vancouver, Toronto, and Montreal were statistically more likely to live in apartments than in detached houses (more the norm in cities like Calgary and Edmonton). Apartment dwellers like Hugh and Aisha were learning a new model of family life, different from the residential neighbourhood model of previous generations.

One characteristic of that model was that people usually knew their neighbours. It's different for today's parents. From my conversations, I came to conclude that, regardless of their geographic location or type of housing, they—and their children—were isolated in a way that was consequential. Not knowing the neighbours links to the issues of risk I raised earlier; children are much more constrained in neighbourhoods their parents perceive to be unsociable, and (therefore) risky. What so often seems to happen is that they are kept indoors, and driven everywhere when they are outdoors. Parents are indoors too—or driving.

In conclusion . . .

The discussion has now come full circle; neighbourhood isolation is part of a much bigger, linked set of problems that have emerged again and again in the previous chapters. Parents are driving because they, and their children, are busy. (In several conversations, parents remarked on the shortage of down time, for everyone.) Often there isn't the time to cultivate the relationships that would give them support. And the geographic mobility that is characteristic of today's parents often also means they don't live close to family members—the people from whom help might be most forthcoming. With rare exceptions, the parents I spoke with had few people around to help them—and most of them could have used some help. Families where parents were employed full-time were the busiest and the most stressed. Workplaces usually offered little flexibility or support, and family responsibilities were now part of that other high-performance job—the one called *parenting*.

I began this project to explore how things had changed for the parents of children in Canada today, to find out what the contemporary "culture of parenting" was like. I found most of my answer in three issues: the heavy expectations now placed on parents, and parents alone, to achieve specified, standardized (and not always realistic) outcomes for their children; the surveillance and the judging, in both the real and the virtual worlds, that together seek to ensure those expectations are met; and the social isolation that sees parents often struggling on their own to do what they hope is the right thing. There is competition and guilt, and, when it comes to children, a lack of trust between adults that means very little help is either offered or solicited. Heather, introduced in Chapter 5, had a comment worth repeating here: "Society doesn't feel accommodating sometimes to parents, and then that leaves us isolated. . . . It leaves parents having to do it all. And it's so hard. Even though you love [your children] so much, you get so worn down." As I noted in the introduction, the UK scholar Frank Furedi calls this is "the breakdown of adult solidarity."

This chapter set out to tell "the story so far." To judge from all the foregoing, it is not a good news story. But neither is it the whole story. Many of the contemporary challenges of child-rearing raised here are meeting with resistance. In many areas, change is, if not actually afoot, at least visible on the horizon. The next chapter describes some of these signs of change, and the possibility of a "culture of parenting" that is not so hard on parents.

8

Imagining the future

In all the discussion in previous chapters about the raising of children, the group that has not so far been consulted directly about the undertaking—even though its members are key players—is children. When they *are* consulted, they have a great deal to contribute.

Few scholars have made this more clear than the US sociologist of childhood William Corsaro.[1] His research with children, in the US, Italy, and Norway, has enabled him to challenge old views of children as passive objects of socialization by adults. In fact Corsaro wants to abandon the notion of socialization, in favour of an understanding of children as active participants in learning about the world—as "beings," not "becomings." He came to this conclusion, in a series of ethnographic research studies, by joining children in the spaces where they played, quietly observing, participating in their conversations if he was invited, and recording what he observed. His work beautifully illuminates how children process, in their own peer culture, what they pick up from adults and the world around them—how they practise, modify and make sense of it. As they do so, they learn so much, and they learn it without being "taught."

"The little chairs" routine is a charming example, emerging from research done by Corsaro and a colleague in a nursery school in Italy. It took place in a large room, in which there were many children's chairs that they sat on for various activities, and it was created entirely by the children. One child would begin it by pushing chairs to the centre of the room. Other children joined in, and a line of chairs was formed. The next stage was for each participating child to climb on to the first chair, and then step from chair to chair along the line. Corsaro notes that the routine took a slightly different form every day over the course of the school year, but some rules were always followed. The chairs were always spaced so that the children could easily step from one to another, and they didn't allow chairs to be removed from the finished structure. Older children reprimanded younger children who didn't always follow the rules, and they sought to reassure the teachers whom they knew were worried about their safety. When falls did occur, they comforted one another. Near the end of the year, some of the older children started to experiment with the design of the structure, to make it more challenging to walk on. Corsaro enumerates many outcomes of routines like these, but one clear message to adults is that children live in their own world, as well as the world of their parents. Parents don't teach them everything they know.

Corsaro's understanding of children as independent and active learners is shared by US developmental psychologist Alison Gopnik, introduced in the previous chapter. Gopnik comes to this conclusion on the basis of extensive research—her own and others'—with babies and toddlers. She paints a fascinating picture of the ways they learn—through looking, listening, and what she calls "the work of play." Like many of the parent educators described in earlier chapters, Gopnik notes the remarkable brain development that happens in children's early years. But the compelling, empirically based argument she makes is that it will happen without the conscious intervention of parents. "Parents and other caregivers don't have to teach young children so much as they just have to let them learn," she says.[2]

This is not to suggest that intervention isn't sometimes needed, in cases where family troubles or serious developmental delays require special help. But what Gopnik's work suggests is that, for most children and most parents, another approach might be possible. In most cases parents could be doing less, not more.

Replacing "parenting"

Gopnik understands where the "parenting" model has come from. She notes that smaller families, greater mobility and older first-time parents have "radically altered the learning curve." Where not so long ago people grew up in large families, and got plenty of experience caring for children before they became parents themselves, today's parents don't have access to that "wisdom and competence." They look to all the parenting advice to fill the gap.[3]

Gopnik's extended argument is that the "parenting" model of raising children runs counter to what children need in order to learn and grow. That model, for Gopnik, sees parents *directing* children's learning, almost as if they were in school, when in fact so much of what they learn comes from many other sources. In the previous chapter I noted her concern that "parenting" turns parents into "carpenters," intent on shaping each child into some idealized vision of the adult that they want the child to become. Instead, she argues, what children need are parents who are "gardeners," who will create a protected and nurturing space where children can flourish—where they can look and listen, and do the work of play. As gardeners, parents play a role quite different from that proposed by the "parenting" model. It's hard work, too, and (like work in any garden) will often be messy. But in Gopnik's view, it is much better than the alternative. She considers that "parenting" hasn't improved the lives of parents and children—and can't actually be shown to have long-term beneficial effects. She notes:

> [It] is very difficult to find any reliable, empirical relation between the small variations in what parents do—the variations that are the focus of parenting—and the resulting adult traits of their children. There is very little evidence that conscious decisions about co-sleeping or not, letting your children "cry it out" or holding them till they fall asleep, or forcing them to do extra homework or letting them play have reliable and predictable long-term effects on who those children become. From an empirical perspective, parenting is a mug's game.[4]

Many of the parents I spoke with had discovered that "parenting" was a mug's game from a practical perspective as well. I noted in Chapter 5 the strong message, in many conversations, about the need to ignore advice and do what worked—in individual and sometimes changing circumstances, and with children who were uniquely themselves. Francine's comment was typical: "At some point I really did overkill, in terms of information. And with time I realized it's about fit, there's no theory that will work with my child. My child is very different than other children, so it's what works for us." Kate said: "I think you can want to do everything the best that you can, and then get kind of bogged down with that. . . . Sometimes you just have to be good enough." Jane added: "I feel like I can trust my instincts. I feel like I have good kids."

If parents like these three wanted support for their positions, they would be able to find it, not only from scholars like Gopnik and Corsaro, but in a whole other category of "parenting advice." In Chapter 1 I noted some of the Canadian contributions to this field—for example from clinical psychologist Alex Russell, whose book *Drop the Worry Ball* encourages parents to relinquish some of the heavy responsibility they feel for every aspect of their children's lives, or from developmental psychologist Gordon Neufeld, who is scathing about the parenting advice industry that, he claims, is robbing parents of their natural competence. And though as I also noted there is a certain irony in the fact that all this professional encouragement to resist advice comes in the form of more advice—or at any rate more reading material—it is advice intended to reassure parents, rather than worry them. Doing less, rather than more, might liberate them from many "shoulds" of the "parenting" model, and perhaps more often allow them to enjoy their children in the present moment.

Reframing risk

One morning in August, 2016, I was in the vicinity of a group of parents who seemed to be doing just that. I was at a mobile adventure playground in a Calgary park, watching a circle of preschoolers sitting around a big log, learning to hammer nails. A play worker was present, but the kids were working on their own. I was especially struck by a little boy, probably no older than 4, patiently trying to make his nail stand up straight, as he got in a few blows. Then he would rest and adjust his hammer hold, and pound some more. I was sure he would quit before he got the nail in—it was quite a long one, and he had been at it for some time. But he didn't quit. He worked away till the job was done. It was a delight to watch.

The hammering was only a small part of what was happening on the playground. The play materials were unconventional—planks, tires, lengths of rope, big wooden spools, huge cardboard and other boxes, lengths of plastic pipe that children could climb through, even an old bathtub. There were about 20 children playing during the time I was there. Some of them were crawling through the plastic pipes, giving one another rolling rides in them, then filling them up with tires and pieces of wood (and occasionally barring entry on the grounds that whatever was going on inside was "under construction"). It was exactly the sort of play with which Corsaro would have been familiar, and which Gopnik would have encouraged. As I wrote in my fieldnotes, "I had forgotten, till I watched these kids, just how creative and imaginative kids at play can be. So many good (and, this morning, visible, demonstrable) reasons for parents to sit back. To their credit, in almost every case, they did. There were lots of picnic blankets and parents (mostly moms) parked outside the circle. The kids had pretty free rein inside."

The mobile playground (which rotated through several city parks) was run by Calgary's municipal parks and recreation department. It was piloted during the summers of 2016 and 2017, as part of a broader initiative which also involved two parent surveys, and formal observation of some 350 children aged between 5 and 12 as they played. One of the surveys, described in the previous chapter, was intended to gauge parents' perceptions of the barriers to free unstructured play for their children, with the goal of making it more available—and commonplace. As I noted in Chapter 7, parents identified many constraints, including time availability, risk and safety factors, and concern about surveillance. But almost to a person, they could see the value of such play, and *wanted* their children to be doing it. The second survey sought parents' views on the adventure playgrounds. A report on that survey[5] notes that feedback was "overwhelmingly positive." There was also extensive, and positive, media coverage.[6] Concerned that descriptions of play as "risky" might evoke connotations of hazard or danger instead of adventure, city officials billed the playground as an "adventure" playground, and the parents' survey referred only to "unstructured" or "outdoor" play. But play containing elements of risk was what was on offer.

The Calgary initiative was funded by a grant from the Lawson Foundation,[7] part of a $2.7 million funding package to 18 projects across the country, in support of the Foundation's Outdoor Play Strategy. The goal of the strategy is to support work with community organizations, researchers, and shapers of public policy (like the City of Calgary) to produce tools, resources and training in support of unstructured outdoor play—the kind of play that may not be "as safe as possible," but that can be used to help children experience and manage risk appropriate to their years. The underlying assumption is that Canadian children need this kind of play, which all the evidence suggests they are experiencing less and less. The position statement developed by researchers involved in the early stages of the strategy makes this position clear: "Access to active play in nature and outdoors—with its risks—is essential for healthy child development. We recommend increasing children's opportunities for self-directed play outdoors in all settings—at home, at school, in child-care, the community and nature."[8] The Canadian Public Health Association, another Lawson Foundation beneficiary, has issued a similar statement. Its funding will be used to address risk concerns and their influence on insurance liability and tort law. The resulting toolkit should be applicable to urban and rural communities.

The Lawson Foundation strategy, and the projects it is supporting, may be among the clearest signs of a shift in thinking in Canada about children and risk—risk being the inevitable accompaniment of free, unstructured play. The benefits to children's development is certainly acknowledged by many of the researchers introduced in Chapter 7, key among them being Mariana Brussoni at the University of British Columbia. She too has received some funding from the Lawson Foundation, and has developed an engaging online tool (called OutsidePlay.ca) to help parents and caregivers "gain the confidence to allow their kids to engage in more outdoor play."[9] There is evidence now that this shift in thinking is shaping plans for parks and playgrounds in municipalities across the country. [10]

Yet another recipient of funding is the Child and Nature Alliance of Canada, which will work to provide support and training for educators to work in forest schools. Forest schools, of the kind attended by several of the Calgary children whose parents I introduced in Chapters 5 and 6, offer opportunities for children of all ages to learn outdoors in nature, using a play- and inquiry-based approach. The first forest school was opened in Canada in 2008. There are now 41 across the country, and in some jurisdictions they are part of the public education system.[11]

I was drawn to find out more about forest schools after catching sight of a group of children playing in the undeveloped parkland near the river where I live. Though I didn't know it at the time, it happened to be the site of the forest school I described in Chapter 6, in which Debra and Cam had registered their children. I was on the much-used walking path through the park, and was so surprised to see children playing there that I followed up. The point here is that we *don't* see children playing outside as a regular occurrence. If the push for more unstructured outdoor play takes effect, it may happen more often.

Changing communities

In the short term, at least, a push for more outdoor play might get parents outdoors too. I noted earlier the parental presence at the adventure play-ground I visited. If strategies like Brussoni's online program, described earlier, persuade parents of the benefits of outdoor play, then we might also see more of them watching kids climbing trees in parks and digging in the dirt in their front yards. We certainly should see more children outdoors. If the Ottawa Student Transportation Authority model of walk-ing school buses[12] is taken up in other communities, we might see more children walking to school—perhaps initially with paid supervisors (as is the case in some of the Ottawa schools). Getting children to school by means other than driving them would have the dual effects of reducing traffic—the source of many parental fears—and getting both children and parents to experience their neighbourhoods in new ways. In research on parents' transportation choices in four Vancouver neighbourhoods, sociol-ogist Arlene Tigar McLaren found that, though there were many inequi-ties behind these choices (poor parents often had few options), there were also signs that change in the direction of less driving was possible.[13] If it happened, it would change many neighbourhood environments.

These sorts of transformations are complicated. Issues like traffic man-agement and urban design involve municipal authorities as well. But here too there are signs of change. Another dimension of the Lawson Foun-dation grant to the City of Calgary was the creation of a play charter, co-signed by 36 community organizations, signalling an increased commit-ment to providing spaces and opportunities for outdoor unstructured play in city neighbourhoods. A model on a much larger scale could be the new policy on play just announced by the (UK) City of London. The London policy states that "development proposals for schemes that are likely to be used by children and young people should increase opportunities for play and informal recreation and enable children and young people to be independently mobile" and that "large scale public realm developments should incorporate incidental play space to make the space more play-able."[14] Urban planning initiatives like the City of Toronto's *Growing Up: Planning for Children in New Vertical Communities*, described in Chapter 2, share many of the Calgary and London goals of increasing play space for children and allowing them to be more independently mobile.

The visibility of children outdoors might go some way towards changing the "community norms" noted in the last chapter by the Calgary survey respondent, whose child was the only one walking to school. The effect might be to moderate the surveillance so many parents fear; there is strength, as well as safety, in numbers. Giving neighbours the opportunity to *see* children climbing trees might also modify perceptions of risk. As another survey respondent commented: "Other parents, our society in general, need to understand that kids are capable of independence, are responsible and that giving kids the freedom to for example, go the park on their own actually enhances their decision making competence. Parents may have forgotten how to play and may need support to learn how to encourage play in their children."

But getting children active outdoors, especially if they are not being directly supervised, requires a level of trust in others that often isn't there. Getting to know the neighbours was a challenge for many of the parents I spoke with. It linked to the problem of social isolation that I felt many of them experienced. On the basis of his extensive work with children and families, it is a concern that Corsaro raises too. Children, he says, "need more opportunities and space to collectively 'weave their webs' with others"[15]—in their own families, and in peer, school, and neighbourhood cultures. Parents like Trevor and Karen, introduced in Chapter 5, were intentional about making neighbourhood connections. So was Terry, the father whose family delivered Christmas cookies up and down the street. But it was difficult for many other parents, especially when working lives left little time to be sociable.

Community organizations—like libraries[16] and parks departments—are stepping up to provide play opportunities for children that parents on their own find difficult. But other organizations are working on a different track, to provide more community connections for parents. Programs for parents and children in family support organizations were critically important for parents like Andrea and Clive, introduced in earlier chapters, who were exceptionally isolated. Other versions of community building are also worth considering. For example, the City of Edmonton's community services department supports a grassroots movement called the Abundant Community Initiative, based on the work of US community activists John McKnight and Peter Block.[17] The approach sees volunteers working on a block-by-block basis, connecting with neighbours and finding out about their needs and their interests. Block connectors work with

a neighbourhood connector, who pools this informal "human resources" information and puts people in touch with one another. In a blog post,[18] Anne Harvey, the co-ordinator of the City's initiative, was quoted as saying that it was "growing like wildfire." She commented: "Within a few weeks in Highlands [the neighbourhood in which the initiative was launched] there was a new moms' group meeting in members' homes so their kids could play together. They share tips and tactics about parenthood, and they often babysit for each other."

Other initiatives to facilitate in-person connections between parents are the work of individuals, or groups of individuals. A remarkable resource to get fathers together in London, Ontario, is the group called Dad Club London. Founded in 2013 by two fathers, it operates as "the go-to resource for fathers and pending fathers, where they can network with other like-minded dads, give and receive help, and become more involved in their community."[19] It now has nearly 3,000 members, and has inspired a sister club of nearly 5,000 moms. The difference between Dad Club London and other online networks is that it is local. Several of the fathers I spoke with were members, and attested to its usefulness in bringing dads together. A recently developed app (called Social.mom) to help mothers find other mothers in their neighbourhoods operates along similar lines. The app's developer, Audrey Poulin, notes on her website[20] her personal experience of being alone as a new mother, and the immeasurable difference made by in-person contact with other mothers.

All of these initiatives encourage people to meet where they live. More in-person contact, between parents perhaps willing to leave the "parenting" model behind and try new things, might expand those parents' tolerance for different approaches, and make everyone less judgmental. Neighbourhoods might start to feel different too.

Work, families, and time

Neighbourhood sociability takes time to set up, and time to experience. And by now the point has been made repeatedly that time is in short supply for many parents. The time constraints experienced by many of those I spoke with represent a problem that Corsaro also identified as getting in the way of children's well-being. In many ways this is a more intractable problem, because it has multiple roots. Corsaro names workplace flexibility and the availability of good quality child-care as key issues, but in many cases it's even more complicated. The workplaces most likely to be flexible are also likely to be the workplaces of professional employees whose jobs carry over into after-hours work online. And as Chapter 2 noted, a high proportion of Canadian employees are in precarious work in which "flexibility" might translate to no work at all. Tolerance for less than satisfactory working conditions is also more likely in cities like Vancouver and Toronto where housing prices make enormous financial demands. And the absence of affordable child-care, noted in Chapter 2, shapes the work decisions of parents across the country. Many Canadian parents simply can't afford to work less.

There are some signs of change—though for many workers they are distant hopes rather than present help. Two are contained in the 2017 federal budget. The first would allow federally regulated workers to request flexible work arrangements from their employers.[21] That could include things like the ability to have "flexible start and finish times and the ability to work from home." Though this change would apply only to workers governed by the Canada Labour Code, it may be the start of further change. Nora Spinks, the executive director of the Vanier Institute of the Family, has been quoted as saying that, though the federal government can't mandate provinces to change their legislation, federal and provincial legislation tends to harmonize over time. The changes mean that the federal government "set a new bar that provincial legislation may rise to," if it doesn't already exceed it. Spinks noted that some collective agreements, which supersede both federal and provincial legislation, might also see the new federal flex work rules as a benchmark.[22]

The second change heralded in the 2017 budget involves extra funding—an additional $7 billion over 10 years, starting in 2018–19—to support and create more high-quality, affordable child-care spaces across the country. A portion of this investment will be dedicated to early learning and child-care programs for Indigenous children living on- and off-reserve.[23] This initiative is intended to address the shortage of affordable child-care spaces noted earlier, which exists everywhere except Quebec. (Quebec's child-care policy could in fact be a model for the rest of Canada). And though critics suggest the current federal initiatives do not go far enough,[24] they also acknowledge that to have the federal government at the table to work on child-care issues is a good sign. Provinces have also begun to take action on child-care. For example, in April 2017 the

Government of Alberta announced pilot project funding to 22 early learning and child-care centres that would offer $25-a-day child-care for nearly 1,300 children.[25]

The other link to parental work stress is the issue of housing. Here too another federal initiative might be cause for (distant) hope. In November 2017 the federal government announced its national housing policy, which includes $40 billion over 10 years to support the creation of affordable housing, and provide rent subsidies among other initiatives. As part of the policy, the Canada Housing Benefit will be launched in 2020, "to provide support directly to families and individuals in housing need, including those currently living in social housing, those on a social housing wait-list and those housed in the private market but struggling to make ends meet." [26]

Parents like Kyle, introduced in Chapter 2, struggling with the high cost of housing in Vancouver, are definitely in the latter category. They're the focus of a research project called "Generation Squeeze," also introduced in Chapter 2. Described as a national collaboration to represent millennials in politics and the marketplace, its "new deal for families" proposes 18 months of affordable, shareable parental leave, $10-a-day child-care, and modified work arrangements that would allow a couple to get by on a 70-hour work week. Generation Squeeze actively lobbies on behalf of its constituents; a blog post[27] noted recent meetings in Ottawa with parliamentarians connected to the main areas of Generation Squeeze concern.

Getting support

What would help, in any of the circumstances I've mentioned, is more support to parents. Here many threads come together. Institutional support from workplaces and government programs, combined with community and personal efforts to combat social isolation, would all contribute to making parents' lives easier.

The first place to check on the availability of help is right inside the home. I've noted in earlier chapters that, statistically speaking, mothers as a group tend to be the most burdened—not only with the actual physical work of child-rearing, but also by the expectations of "intensive mothering" that the current climate of "parenting" heaps on them. The mothers I spoke with who were the most distressed were those with husbands who were not engaged with their children, and offered little or no physical help. There were only a handful of fathers like this, and I heard about them only second-hand. The fathers I spoke with myself were (not surprisingly, given their interest in my project) quite different. Most seemed to be as involved with caregiving as their partners were. On the basis of my own past research,[28] which had focused on just such engaged fathers, I was not surprised by what I was hearing in these more recent conversations. But it was something of a shock to hear that the unhelpful kind were still out there.

The hope here has to be that fathers generally *are* becoming more involved, as I noted in Chapter 2. And those who are model that behavior to others. (Alan made the point bluntly: "I am still astounded when I go somewhere, and the baby has a dirty diaper, and the dad hands it to the mom. I just want to get up and smack him . . . 'What makes you so special? I did three thousand of those.'") The 2018 federal budget, which provides fathers and other non-birth parents five weeks of "use-it-or-lose-it" parental leave (starting June 2019) may give more fathers the hands-on caregiving experience Alan was talking about. (A similar – though somewhat more generous – policy in Quebec has had just this effect.)[29]

Child-rearing pressures were alleviated for some lucky parents by the presence of grandparents able to step in and help, with emotional support, and also with child-care. I noted in earlier chapters that it was this family support that parents valued, and missed when it was not available. I also noted a widespread reluctance among many to ask for help from friends. It's here that change might have the most effect. As some of the community initiatives noted earlier also suggest, connection and support might be more available than many parents think—if only they are trusting enough to ask for it. Like Nadie, the Indigenous mother introduced in Chapter 6, they'll also be asked somewhere along the way to give help, as well as receive it. But the web of reciprocal sharing and care that would result would go a long way to rebuilding the adult solidarity described as a casualty of contemporary family life. This is not to suggest that those networks of support were unknown among the parents I spoke with. There were some heartwarming stories of friendship groups extended to include children when they arrived (as happened for Bruce), or reworked when some of the early stresses were overcome. The passage of time made it possible for Michelle to reconnect with the friends whose perceived "perfect mothering" in the early years had scared her away. "We all loosened up," she said. The point is, though, that parents do have to seek out these connections, and the help they can provide, because they need them. As Samantha said: "Parenting is great . . . but it requires the input of many, many people."

In conclusion . . .

I began this chapter with a discussion of children, because of the place they have in the future we are imagining. If we are looking for ways to make parents' experience less stressful, the way we think about children is a good place to start. Scholars like Corsaro and Gopnik point out that children may not need quite as much from parents as we think they do. Or rather, they need something different—gardening rather than carpentry. And though gardening is hard work, it doesn't come with the heavy burden of expectations that carpenters face. I want to suggest that, though it's a bit of a simplification, parents can be gardeners by *being* parents, not by *doing* parenting.

Moving away from the "parenting" model requires other shifts in thinking—about children and risk, as a starting point. While the discussion of risk in this chapter has focused on changing approaches to children's play, these changes underlie a powerful shift in thinking about what children are capable of. When they are perceived as less vulnerable and fragile, they can be allowed more free rein in the outside world—and that, in turn, has profound implications.

Children out in the world will call on parents to be much more trusting of neighbours and others than has been the case for quite some time. Distrust has isolated them in their neighbourhoods and communities. They are often isolated too because, unlike the parents of generations past, they are much less likely to live in familiar settings, near other family members. I have suggested some of the strategies in place to address the social isolation of many parents. And I have noted the changes that might address some of the time challenges that all parents, but particularly employed parents, face on a daily basis.

Many of these changes may seem, at best, hopes for a future a long way down the road. Pessimists may see them as whistling in the dark. But I find pessimism to be unhelpful. US journalist Jennifer Senior described raising children today as "all joy and no fun." This book has certainly confirmed that it is hard work for most parents. But I hope it can also contribute to a conversation about doing it differently, to make it easier—and more fun.

Endnotes

Introduction

1 https://www.today.com/parents/mom-responds-after-investigation-over-kids-playing-yard-i-am-t88521 Retrieved Feb. 19, 2018.

2 Nelson, 2010: 1. Faircloth also uses Nelson's reflections in the way I use them here. See Faircloth 2014a: 25.

3 Lee, Ellie, Jennie Bristow, Charlotte Faircloth, and Jan Macvarish. 2014. *Parenting Culture Studies*. Houndmills, Basingstoke: Palgrave Macmillan.

4 Furedi 2002.

5 Lee 2014: 9–10.

6 But see for example Faircloth et al. 2013.

7 http://www.humanservices.alberta.ca/family-community/15575.html Retrieved May 19, 2016.

8 Probably needless to say, this perspective on parenting relates to economically privileged countries. Within those countries, though, as I will show in later discussion, dominant ideas about parenting may profoundly affect less privileged members.

9 Hunt 2003: 167–68.

10 My discussion draws directly on Lee 2014: 10–16.

11 See 2016 Canadian Centre for Child Protection report: https://www.protectchildren.ca/app/en/amc.

12 Lee 2014: 12.

13 Thomas et al. 2016.

14 The CBC program segment can be accessed at http://www.cbc.ca/listen/shows/the-current/segment/10730968 Retrieved August 4, 2017.

15 Lee 2014: 15.

16 This field in sociology, on the construction of social problems, is represented in Lee's discussion by researchers such as Best (1993, 1995).

17 Lee 2014: 18–19.

18 See for example http://www.hc-sc.gc.ca/fn-an/nutrition/infant-nourisson/index-eng.php (on breastfeeding) and http://www.phac-aspc.gc.ca/hp-gs/guide/03_ap-ag-eng.php (on alcohol consumption during pregnancy). Retrieved Nov. 25, 2017.

19 See for example Bruer (1999), Bruner (2000), Gopnik (2016).

20   Macvarish 2016: 2.

21   Wall 2004. See also Wall (2010).

22   Hays 1996: 8.

23   Canadian Child Welfare Research portal, http://cwrp.ca/sites/default/files/publications/en/144e.pdf Retrieved Nov. 25, 2017

24   See for example Elkind (2007); Guldberg (2009); Gopnik (2016).

25   Louv 2008.

26   See for example Mose (2016).

27   See for example the 2016 Pew Research Center report, retrieved Nov. 25, 2017, from http://www.pewinternet.org/2016/01/07/parents-teens-and-digital-monitoring. Note also companies now marketing "parental control software" – for example http://www.fsm.de/youth-protection/parental-control-software.

28   Bristow 2014.

29   See for example Mintz (2004).

30   See for example Corsaro (2009). See also Charles (2011), Charles et al. (2010, 2012) and Liegghio (2015) on older children's roles as carers and support-providers in some vulnerable families.

31   Bristow 2014: 200.

32   See https://www.washingtonpost.com/posteverything/wp/2015/01/16/i-let-my-9-year-old-ride-the-subway-alone-i-got-labeled-the-worlds-worst-mom/. Retrieved Nov. 25, 2017. See also Skenazy (2009).

33   *All Joy and No Fun: The Paradox of Modern Parenthood* is the title of Senior's 2014 book.

34   Senior 2014: 238–39.

35   Senior 2014: 7.

36   http://www.statcan.gc.ca/pub/11-630-x/11-630-x2016005-eng.htm Retrieved Dec. 8, 2017.

37   http://www.statcan.gc.ca/pub/89-503-x/2015001/article/14694-eng.htm Retrieved Dec. 8, 2017.

38   https://www.statcan.gc.ca/pub/75-006-x/2015001/article/14202/parent-eng.htm Retrieved Dec. 8, 2017.

Chapter 1

1   Spock 1979.

2   Pace 1998. http://www.nytimes.com/learning/general/onthisday/bday/0502.html Retrieved July 24, 2017.

3   Sociologist Katherine Arnup notes the significance of Spock's contributions in a historical survey of advice to Canadian mothers. See Arnup (1994).

4   My source for these changes is an exhaustive historical study of parenting ad-

vice by Hardyment (1983).

5   Knaak 2005.

6   Quirke 2006.

7   Wall 2013.

8   http://www.phac-aspc.gc.ca/hp-gs/guide/assets/pdf/hpguide-eng.pdf Retrieved July 16, 2017.

9   A baby's birth is also the source of a vast amount of formal and informal advice. Since my focus is on what happens when the baby arrives, I am deliberately bypassing the birthing material.

10   https://www.canada.ca/en/health-canada/services/food-nutrition/healthy-eating/infant-feeding/nutrition-healthy-term-infants-recommendations-birth-six-months/6-24-months.html Retrieved July 17, 2017.

11   https://www.canada.ca/en/health-canada/services/consumer-product-safety/reports-publications/consumer-education/your-child-safe/sleep-time.html Retrieved Feb. 17, 2018

12   http://www.child-encyclopedia.com/sites/default/files/docs/coups-oeil/brain-development-in-children-structure-info.pdf Retrieved August 3, 2017.

13   See for example Thornton (2011); Hoffman (2010); Kanieski (2010).

14   Wall (forthcoming).

15   http://www2.gov.bc.ca/gov/content/family-social-supports/caring-for-young-children/how-parents-can-support-young-children Retrieved July 17, 2017.

16   http://www.gov.mb.ca/healthychild/ecd/ Retrieved July 19, 2017.

17   From the website of Family Resource Programs Canada (http://www.frp.ca/index.cfm?fuseaction=Page.viewPage&pageId=473) Retrieved July 19, 2017.

18   http://www.cps.ca/en/documents/position/screen-time-and-young-children Retrieved July 19, 2017.

19   https://www.participaction.com/en-ca/thought-leadership/playdate-and-guidelines/0-4. Retrieved Nov. 20, 2017.

20   See for example http://www.cbc.ca/news/health/toddlers-babies-exercise-guidelines-1.4410276. Retrieved Nov. 20, 2017.

21   https://www.learnalberta.ca/content/mychildslearning/ Retrieved July 20, 2017.

22   https://news.gov.bc.ca/releases/2017EDUC0091-001075 Retrieved July 20, 2017.

23   https://www.participaction.com/sites/default/files/downloads/2016%20ParticipACTION%20Report%20Card%20-%20Full%20Report.pdf Retrieved July 20, 2017.

24   http://www.cheo.on.ca/en/physicalpunishment Retrieved July 22, 2017.

25   Sanders and Turner 2016: 229. Dr. Matthew Sanders is the Director of the Parenting and Family Support Centre at the University of Queensland, and the founder of Triple P.

26   See for example Ponzetti (2016); Benzies and Barker (2016).

27   http://www12.statcan.gc.ca/census-recensement/2016/dp-pd/hlt-fst/fam/Table.cfm?Lang=E&T=41&Geo=00 Retrieved August 3, 2017.

28   Lee et al. 2014.

29   Baker et al. 2017: 916.

30   http://www.triplep-parenting.ca/can-en/triple-p/ Retrieved July 22, 2017.

31   http://www.parentsmatter.ca/index.cfm?fuseaction=page.viewPage&pageID=600 Retrieved July 28, 2017.

32   It's important to note that a small, but dwindling, proportion of Canadians don't have home internet access. The latest available Statistics Canada survey set the proportion at 17 percent of households in 2012, and noted that most were low-income households (see http://www.statcan.gc.ca/daily-quotidient/131126/dq131126d-eng.htm, retrieved August 3, 2017). However I think my focus on online material can be justified by the fact that the vast majority of households do have internet access.

33   http://www.statcan.gc.ca/daily-quotidien/131126/dq131126d-eng.htm Retrieved Aug 3, 2017.

34   Fréchette and Romano 2015.

35   Gulli 2017. http://www.macleans.ca/society/the-collapse-of-parenting-why-its-time-for-parents-to-grow-up/ Retrieved July 28, 2017.

36   http://www.macleans.ca/society/cover-preview-cathy-gulli-on-the-collapse-of-parenting/ Retrieved July 28, 2017.

37   https://www.facebook.com/macleans/photos/a.10150173658593950.324988.8529948949/10153793761198950/?type=3&hc_ref=PAGES_TIMELINE Retrieved July 28, 2017.

38   http://www.macleans.ca/society/live-chat-leonard-sax-on-the-collapse-of-parenting/ Retrieved July 28, 2017.

39   Sax 2016.

40   Neufeld and Maté 2013.

41   http://neufeldinstitute.org/about-us/who-we-are/ Retrieved August 1, 2017.

42   Pickert 2012. http://time.com/606/the-man-who-remade-motherhood/ Retrieved Sept. 19, 2017.

43   Sears et al. 2013. See also Sears and Sears (2001).

44   https://www.askdrsears.com/topics/parenting/attachment-parenting Retrieved July 31, 2017.

45   See Rippeyoung (2013a).

46   Ferber 2006. See also an interview with Ferber, and comments, at http://www.parenting.com/article/the-truth-about-ferberizing Retrieved August 3, 2017.

47   See for example http://www.justthefactsbaby.com/baby/article/when-to-start-sleep-training-105/page=3, and http://www.huffingtonpost.ca/dr-dina-kulik/sleep-training-methods_b_5582968.html. Retrieved Feb. 19, 2018.

48   See for example Rippeyoung (2013b).

49 http://www.cbc.ca/news/health/breast-feeding-formula-feeding-depression-lactation-clinics-1.3995075 Retrieved August 2, 2017.

50 http://www.huffingtonpost.ca/2017/01/18/florence-leung-husband-death-postpartum-breastfeeding_n_14235480.html Retrieved July 31, 2017.

51 https://fedisbest.org/

52 https://www.acog.org/Resources-And-Publications/Committee-Opinions/Committee-on-Obstetric-Practice/Optimizing-Support-for-Breastfeeding-as-Part-of-Obstetric-Practice. Retrieved Feb. 19, 2018.

53 See for example https://www.theglobeandmail.com/life/parenting/the-movement-to-bring-back-risky-play-for-children/article31345490/ Retrieved August 2, 2017.

54 http://www.freerangekids.com/what-is-free-range-parenting-a-primer-from-the-cbc/ Retrieved August 2, 2017.

55 http://www.cbc.ca/radio/thecurrent/the-current-for-august-7-2015-1.3182631/free-range-kids-just-the-latest-parenting-trend-1.3182668 See also http://www.cbc.ca/news/canada/british-columbia/america-s-worst-mom-comes-to-b-c-1.3948793 Retrieved August 2, 2017.

56 Hoffman 2010.

57 Camarata 2015.

58 Hurley 2015.

59 https://www.facebook.com/andrea.m.nair/ Retrieved August 1, 2017.

60 http://www.yummymummyclub.ca/blogs/andrea-nair-button-pushing Retrieved August 1, 2017.

61 http://www.yummymummyclub.ca/blogs/andrea-nair-connect-four-parenting/20151027/apps-for-helping-parents-of-toddlers Retrieved August 1, 2017.

62 http://www.yummymummyclub.ca/blogs/andrea-nair-connect-four-parenting/20170227/parenting-bravely-how-to-increase-our-parenting Retrieved July 29, 2017.

63 http://clca-accl.ca/ This is the website of the Canadian Lactation Consultant Association. Retrieved July 31, 2017.

64 http://babywearingincanada.com/calling-canadian-volunteer-group-leaders/ Retrieved July 31, 2017.

65 https://www.todaysparent.com/baby/does-your-baby-need-a-sleep-coach/ Retrieved July 31, 2017.

66 See for example the Calgary-based parent coaching company Parenting Power: http://parentingpower.ca/about-us/ Retrieved August 1, 2017.

67 http://www.yummymummyclub.ca/our-yummy-team Retrieved July 29, 2017.

68 https://www.facebook.com/pg/DadBloggers/community/?ref=page_internal Retrieved July 31, 2017.

69 Faircloth 2014b.

70 Instagram is a social networking site designed to allow the posting of photos and videos from a smartphone.

71 http://www.huffingtonpost.ca/2015/06/24/ryan-reynolds-instagram-controversy_n_7654300.html Retrieved July 31, 2017.

72 http://blogs.lse.ac.uk/parenting4digitalfuture/2017/05/17/sharenting-in-whose-interests/ See also http://blogs.lse.ac.uk/parenting4digitalfuture/2017/06/06/tiger-mom-2-0-overprinting-for-a-digital-future/ Retrieved August 1, 2017.

73 See also Russell (2015).

74 See for example the blog post and video discussion in the online version of the popular Canadian magazine *Today's Parent*: https://www.todaysparent.com/family/parenting/i-dont-want-to-see-your-kids-rash-why-i-quit-all-facebook-parenting-groups/ Retrieved August 1, 2017. See Grierson (2016) for discussion of shaming in the real, not digital world.

75 Russell 2012: 152 (in online version).

76 See *Today's Parent* link in note 74.

77 Honoré 2008: 3.

78 Russell 2012. See also Honoré (2008).

79 Neufeld and Maté 2013: 55.

Chapter 2

1 Statistics Canada 2015. https://www.statcan.gc.ca/pub/75-006-x/2015001/article/14202/parent-eng.htm Retrieved Dec. 8, 2017.

2 Statistics Canada 2015. http://www.statcan.gc.ca/pub/89-650-x/2012001/tbl/tbl18-eng.htm Retrieved June 7, 2017.

3 Statistics Canada 2017. http://www12.statcan.gc.ca/census-recensement/2016/dp-pd/prof/details/page.cfm?Lang=E&Geo1=PR&Code1=01&-Geo2=&Code2=&Data=Count&SearchText=Canada&SearchType=Begins&-SearchPR=01&B1=All&TABID=1 Retrieved Dec. 8, 2017.

4 Statistics Canada 2015. http://www.statcan.gc.ca/pub/89-650-x/89-650-x2012002-eng.htm Retrieved June 8, 2017.

5 Statistics Canada 2017. http://www.statcan.gc.ca/pub/89-503-x/2015001/article/14694-eng.htm Retrieved Dec. 8, 2017.

6 Lewchuk et. al. 2015. See also Duffy et al. (2015).

7 Premji 2017.

8 Dorow and Mandizadza 2017.

9 See for example Whalen and Schmidt (2016).

10 Duxbury and Higgins 2012. Duxbury interview: http://newsroom.carleton.ca/2012/10/25/carleton-releases-2012-national-study-on-balancing-work-and-caregiving-in-canada-linda-duxbury-to-talk-about-findings-at-building-healthier-workplaces-conference/ Retrieved June 7, 2017.

11 See for example Luxton and Corman (2001); Fox (2009).

12 See for example Doucet (2006); Ranson (2010, 2015).

13 Battams 2017b.

14 Battams 2017b.

15 McKay et al. 2016.

16 For example see Dengate (2016).

17 McKay et al. 2016.

18 Friendly et al. 2015.

19 Battams 2017a.

20 McDonald and Friendly 2016.

21 Zilio 2017. https://www.theglobeandmail.com/news/politics/ottawa-signs-child-care-deal-targeting-families-in-need/article35285367/ Retrieved March 1, 2018

22 Statistics Canada 2015. http://www.statcan.gc.ca/pub/89-652-x/89-652-x2014005-eng.htm Retrieved Feb. 17, 2018.

23 Battams 2016.

24 Ball 2012.

25 Castellano 2002: 16.

26 Thompson et al. 2012.

27 Statistics Canada 2017. http://www.statcan.gc.ca/daily-quotidien/171025/dq171025b-eng.htm Retrieved Dec. 8, 2017.

28 Parsons Leigh, 2016: 1078. See also Bragg and Wong (2016); VanderPlaat et al. (2012); Zhou (2013).

29 Statistics Canada, 2011. http://www.statcan.gc.ca/tables-tableaux/sum-som/l01/cst01/demo62a-eng.htm Retrieved June 11, 2017.

30 Statistics Canada 2017. http://www12.statcan.gc.ca/census-recensement/2016/as-sa/98-200-x/2016005/98-200-x2016005-eng.cfm Retrieved Dec. 8, 2017.

31 Burns, 2017. https://www.thestar.com/life/homes/2017/05/06/why-were-raising-our-kids-in-a-condo.html Retrieved June 12, 2017

32 Statistics Canada 2017. http://www12.statcan.gc.ca/census-recensement/2016/as-sa/98-200-x/2016005/98-200-x2016005-eng.cfm Retrieved Dec. 8, 2017.

33 Lauster, 2016: 180.

34 http://www1.toronto.ca/wps/portal/contentonly?vgnextoid=35cf62e9d-88c0510VgnVCM10000071d60f89RCRD Retrieved June 12, 2017.

35 Torres 2009: 9.

36 Kadane 2013. http://www.calgaryherald.com/news/calgary/School+What+happens+community+when+students+leave+their+neighbourhood+schools/9144683/story.html Retrieved June 12, 2017.

37 http://www.gensqueeze.ca/

Part II

1   Because in some cases these organizations are readily identifiable by location or client base, I am not naming them in order to protect the confidentiality of the people to whom they directed me. But they know who they are, and have already received my grateful thanks.

2   This is less unusual than it might appear; some two-thirds of all Canadians aged 25 to 64 have university or college qualifications. See Statistics Canada 2016. http://www.12.statcan.gc.ca/nhs-enm/2011/as-sa/99-012-x2011001-eng. cfm#a2. Retrieved Dec. 9, 2017.

Chapter 4

1   Currently only Ontario offers universal full-day kindergarten for 4-year-olds, although the Northwest Territories and Nova Scotia plan to follow suit. Full-day kindergarten for 5-year-olds is offered in Newfoundland, P.E.I., Nova Scotia, New Brunswick, Quebec, Ontario, BC, and the Northwest Territories. The rest of the provinces and territories offer part-day kindergarten. See https://theconversation. com/children-gain-learning-boost-from-two-year-full-day-kindergarten-79549 Retrieved Dec. 8, 2017.

2   One mother had a nearly-5-year-old, and a step-child for whom she and her husband cared on a half-time basis.

3   Mothers were pregnant in five of the cases; in the sixth, an adoption was under way.

4   Two of the mothers were a same-sex couple; I spoke with both of them together.

5   As I have noted in the introduction to Part II, the fathers who volunteered for this project are probably not representative of the broader population of fathers.

6   I coined the term "dual dividers" in an earlier project, to describe this kind of sharing. See Ranson 2010.

Chapter 5

1   I will provide more details about forest schools in Chapter 9.

Chapter 6

1   https://globalnews.ca/news/3663732/the-cheapest-and-most-expensive-kids-activities-in-canada-ipsos-poll/ Retrieved Feb. 17, 2018.

Chapter 7

1 http://www.yummymummyclub.ca/blogs/andrea-nair-connect-four-parenting/20151027/apps-for-helping-parents-of-toddlers. Retrieved August 1, 2017.

2 https://www.health.harvard.edu/blog/app-helps-track-developmental-milestones-2017111412718. Retrieved Feb 19, 2018.

3 Valenti 2012.

4 Senior 2014: 238.

5 Wilson et al. 2012; Coyne and Kwakkenbos 2013.

6 Wall (forthcoming).

7 Reece 2013.

8 Macvarish 2016.

9 Thornton 2011.

10 Ramaekers and Suissa 2012: 356.

11 Ibid: 354.

12 Kanieski 2010.

13 Woodhead 2009: 54.

14 Gopnik 2016: 18.

15 See for example Wall (2013).

16 See for example McNamara (2013); Alexander et al. (2014a and b, 2015); Glenn et al. (2012); Berg (2015).

17 Information about the lab, and Brussoni's research, is available at www.brussonilab.ca. Retrieved Nov. 28, 2017.

18 Brussoni and Olsen 2011, 2012.

19 Brunelle et al. 2016; Herrington and Brussoni 2015.

20 Brussoni et al. 2012.

21 See for example Faulkner et al. (2015).

22 Loebach and Gilliland 2016.

23 Ibid.: 447.

24 City of Calgary 2017a.

25 Ibid. See also Tchoukaleyska (2011).

26 Stueck 2017. https://beta.theglobeandmail.com/news/british-columbia/vancouver-man-ordered-to-stop-letting-his-children-take-city-bus-to-school/article36180815/?ref=https://www.theglobeandmail.com&service=mobile. Retrieved Nov. 29, 2017.

27 Thomas et al. 2016.

28 Ibid.: 12.

29 https://www.npr.org/sections/13.7/2016/08/22/490847797/why-do-we-judge-parents-for-putting-kids-at-perceived-but-unreal-risk. Retrieved Nov. 30, 2017.

30 Frønes 2009: 282.

31 See for example http://blogs.lse.ac.uk/parenting4digitalfuture/2017/06/06/tiger-mom-2-0-overprinting-for-a-digital-future/ Retrieved Nov. 30, 2017.

32 See Blackford (2004); Caputo (2007); Tuteur (2016).

33 Lanes et al. 2011.

34 https://psychiatry.ubc.ca/2016/06/24/dr-nichole-fairbrother-in-the-cbc-news-postpartum-anxiety-much-more-common-than-depression-in-new-moms-study-says/ Retrieved Nov. 30, 2017.

35 http://www.huffingtonpost.ca/2017/04/27/postpartum-depression-study_n_16272462.html Retrieved Nov. 30, 2017.

36 Knaak 2009: 80.

37 Ganann et al. 2016.

38 Bragg and Wong 2016.

39 VanderPlaat et al. 2012, Zhou 2013.

40 Alook 2018.

41 See for example Rashi et al. (2015).

42 See for example Malacrida (2007).

Chapter 8

1 Corsaro 2015.

2 Gopnik 2016:145.

3 Ibid.: 21–22.

4 Ibid.: 23.

5 City of Calgary 2017b.

6 See for example http://calgary.ctvnews.ca/new-playground-sparks-kids-imaginations-1.2960784 Retrieved Dec. 6, 2017

7 The Lawson Foundation is a national family philanthropic organization, whose major focus according to its website is "the wellbeing of children and youth." See https://lawson.ca/about-lawson/ Retrieved Dec. 6, 2017.

8 Tremblay et al. 2015: 6475.

9 https://outsideplay.ca/

10 https://www.theglobeandmail.com/news/british-columbia/bc-city-parks-updated-to-reflect-changing-tastes/article37440124/ Retrieved Jan. 31, 2018.

11 http://childnature.ca/about-forest-and-nature-school/ Retrieved Dec. 6, 2017.

12 http://www.cbc.ca/news/canada/ottawa/walking-school-bus-program-can-t-keep-up-with-walking-children-1.3203815 Retrieved Dec. 7, 2017.

13 McLaren and Parusel 2015; McLaren 2016.

14 https://www.childinthecity.org/2017/11/30/new-london-plan-aims-for-more-play-and-mobility-for-children/?utm_source=newsletter&utm_medium=e-mail&utm_campaign=Newsletter%20week%202017-49 Retrieved Dec. 7, 2017.

15 Corsaro 2015: 352.

16 A popular, regularly scheduled event at several Calgary public library branches is the Colossal Calgary Playdate, which draws scores of children to play with indoor versions of the "loose parts" material in adventure playgrounds – materials like shredded paper, cardboard boxes, playdough, and water. Here too, parents mostly stand back and let children play.

17 McKnight and Block 2010. See also the Abundant Community website: http://www.abundantcommunity.com/ Retrieved Dec. 7, 2017.

18 https://transformingedmonton.ca/making-strangers-into-neighbours/ Retrieved Dec. 7, 2017.

19 http://dadclublondon.com/ Retrieved Dec. 8, 2017.

20 https://www.social.mom/en/about

21 https://www.budget.gc.ca/2017/docs/plan/chap-01-en.html#Toc477707320 See also https://globalnews.ca/news/3337525/another-perk-for-parents-from-budget-2017-flexible-work-arrangements/ Retrieved Dec. 8, 2017.

22 https://globalnews.ca/news/3337525/another-perk-for-parents-from-budget-2017-flexible-work-arrangements/ Retrieved Feb. 18, 2018.

23 https://www.budget.gc.ca/2017/docs/plan/chap-02-en.html#Toc477707402 Retrieved Dec. 8, 2017.

24 https://www.thestar.com/news/canada/2017/03/22/federal-budget-money-for-child-care-is-a-good-first-step-but-not-nearly-enough-advocates-say.html Retrieved Dec. 8, 2017.

25 https://www.alberta.ca/release.cfm?xID=46616A6639019-C1E2-0965-1D7AB37C24E9632C Retrieved Dec. 8, 2017.

26 https://www.placetocallhome.ca/pdfs/Canada-National-Housing-Strategy.pdf Retrieved March 1, 2018.

27 https://www.gensqueeze.ca/suit_up_activity_log_ottawa_october_24_27 Retrieved Dec. 8, 2017.

28 Ranson 2010; 2015

29 http://www.cbc.ca/news/canada/toronto/parental-leave-budget-2018-1.4554671 Retrieved March 1, 2018.

Bibliography

Alexander, Stephanie A., Katherine L. Frohlich and Caroline Fusco. 2014a. "Problematizing 'play-for-health' discourses through children's photo-elicited narratives." *Qualitative Health Research* 24(10):1329–41.

—. 2014b. "'Active play may be lots of fun, but it's certainly not frivolous': The emergence of active play as a health practice in Canadian public health." *Sociology of Health and Illness* 36(8):1188–204.

Alexander, Stephanie A., Caroline Fusco and Katherine L. Frohlich. 2015. "'You have to do 60 minutes of physical activity per day . . . I saw it on TV': Children's constructions of play in the context of Canadian public health discourse of playing for health." *Sociology of Health and Illness* 37(2):227–40.

Alook, Angele. 2018 "Indigenous families: Migration, resistance, and resilience." In *Continuity and Innovation: Canadian Families in the New Millennium*, edited by Amber Gazso and Karen Kobayashi. Toronto: Nelson Higher Education.

Arnup, Katherine. 1994. *Education for Motherhood: Advice for Mothers in 20th Century Canada*. Toronto: University of Toronto Press.

Baker, Sabine, Matthew R. Sanders and Alina Morawska. 2017. "Who uses online parenting support? A cross-sectional survey exploring Australian parents' internet use for parenting." *Journal of Child and Family Studies* 26:916–27.

Ball, Jessica. 2012. "'We could be the turn-around generation': Harnessing Aboriginal fathers' potential to contribute to their children's well-being." *Paediatrics and Child Health* 17(7):373–75.

Battams, Nathan. 2016. "Snapshot of grandparents in Canada: Statistical Snapshots." Ottawa: Vanier Institute of the Family.

—. 2017a. "A snapshot of women, work and family in Canada: Statistical Snapshots." Ottawa: Vanier Institute of the Family.

—. 2017b. "A snapshot of men, work and family relationships in Canada: Statistical Snapshots." Ottawa: Vanier Institute of the Family.

Benzies, Karen M. and Leslie A. Barker. 2016. "Program evaluation: What works in parenting education." In *Evidence-Based Parenting Education: A Global Perspective*, edited by James J. Ponzetti Jr. New York: Routledge.

Berg, Stephen. 2015. "Children's activity levels in different playground environments: An observational study in four Canadian preschools." *Early Childhood Education Journal* 43:281–87.

Best, Joel. 1993. *Threatened Children: Rhetoric and Concern about Child Victims*. Chicago: University of Chicago Press.

—. 1995. "Typification and social problem construction." In *Images of Issues*, edited by Joel Best. New York: Aldine de Gruyter.

Blackford, Holly. 2004. "Playground panopticism: Ring-around-the-children, a pocketful of women." *Childhood* 11(2):227–49.

Bragg, Bronwyn and Lloyd L. Wong. 2016. "'Cancelled dreams': Family reunification and shifting Canadian immigration policy." *Journal of Immigrant & Refugee Studies* 14(1):46–65.

Bristow, Jennie. 2014. "Who cares for children? The problem of intergenerational contact." In *Parenting Culture Studies*, edited by Ellie Lee, Jennie Bristow, Charlotte Faircloth and Jan Macvarish. Houndmills, Basingstoke: Palgrave Macmillan.

Bruer, John T. (1999). *The Myth of the First Three Years: A New Understanding of Early Brain Development and Lifelong Learning*. New York: The Free Press.

Brunelle, Sara, Susan Herrington, Ryan Coghlan and Mariana Brussoni. 2016. "Play worth remembering: Are playgrounds too safe?" *Children, Youth and Environments* 26(1):17–36.

Bruner, Jerome. (2000). "Tot thought." In *New York Review of Books*, 47(4), March 9.

Brussoni, Mariana, Lise L. Olsen, Ian Pike and David A. Sleet. 2012. "Risky play and children's safety: Balancing priorities for optimal child development." *International Journal of Environmental Research and Public Health* 9:3134–48.

Brussoni, Mariana and Lise Olsen. 2011. "Striking a balance between risk and protection: Fathers' attitudes and practices towards child injury protection." *Journal of Developmental and Behavioral Pediatrics* 32(7):491–98.

—. 2012. "The perils of overprotective parenting: Fathers' perspectives explored." *Child: Care, Health and Development* 39:237–45.

Burns, Jackie. 2017. "Why we're raising our kids in a condo." In *Toronto Star*. Toronto: Toronto Star Newspapers Ltd. May 6.

Camarata, Stephen. 2015. *The Intuitive Parent: Why the Best Thing for Your*

Child Is You. New York: Current.

Caputo, Virginia. 2007. "She's from a 'good family': Performing childhood and motherhood in a Canadian private school setting." *Childhood* 14(2):173–92.

Castellano, Marlene Brant. 2002. *Aboriginal Family Trends: Extended Families, Nuclear Families, Families of the Heart.* Ottawa: Vanier Institute of the Family.

Charles, Grant, Tim Stainton and Sheila Marshall. 2010. "Young carers in immigrant families: An ignored population." *Canadian Social Work* 12(1):83–92.

Charles, Grant. 2011. "Bringing young carers out of the shadows." *Reclaiming Children and Youth* 20(3):26–30.

Charles, Grant, Tim Stainton and Sheila Marshall. 2012. "Young carers in Canada: The hidden costs and benefits of young caregiving." Ottawa: Vanier Institute of the Family.

City of Calgary: Calgary Parks, Recreation, Business and Market Research. 2017a. "Parental Perceptions of Play: Final Report." Calgary: City of Calgary.

—. 2017b. "2016 Mobile Adventure Playgrounds Pilot: Final Report." Calgary: City of Calgary.

Corsaro, William A. 2009. "Peer culture." *Palgrave Handbook of Childhood Studies*, edited by Jens Qvortrup, William A. Corsaro and Michael-Sebastian Honig. Houndmills, Basingstoke: Palgrave Macmillan.

—. 2015. *The Sociology of Childhood* 4th edn. Los Angeles: Sage

Coyne, James C. and Linda Kwakkenbos. 2013. "Triple P-Positive Parenting programs: The folly of basing social policy on underpowered flawed studies." *BMC Medicine* 11:11.

Dengate, Jennifer. 2016. "How does family policy 'work'? Job context, flexibility and maternity leave policy." *Sociology Compass* 10(5):376–90.

Dorow, Sara and Shingirai Mandizadza. 2017. "Circuits of care: Mobility, work and managing family relationships." Ottawa: Vanier Institute of the Family.

Doucet, Andrea. 2006. *Do Men Mother? Fathering, Care and Domestic Responsibility.* Toronto: University of Toronto Press.

Duffy, Ann, June Corman and Norene Pupo. 2015. "Family finances: Fragility, class, and gender." *Canadian Review of Sociology* 52(2):222–31.

Duxbury, Linda and Chris Higgins. 2012. "Revisiting Work-Life Issues in Canada: The 2012 National Survey on Balancing Work and Caregiving in Canada." Ottawa: Carleton University.

Elkind, David. 2007. *The Power of Play: How Spontaneous, Imaginative Activities Lead to Happier, Healthier Children.* Cambridge MA: Da Capo Press.

Faircloth, Charlotte, Diane M. Hoffman and Linda L. Layne, eds. 2013. *Parenting in Global Perspective.* London and New York: Routledge.

Faircloth, Charlotte. 2014a. "Intensive parenting and the expansion of parenting." In *Parenting Culture Studies*, edited by Ellie Lee, Jennie Bristow, Charlotte Faircloth and Jan Macvarish. Houndmills, Basingstoke: Palgrave Macmillan.

—. 2014b. "The problem of 'attachment': The 'detached' parent." In *Parenting Culture Studies*, edited by Ellie Lee, Jennie Bristow, Charlotte Faircloth and Jan Macvarish. Houndmills, Basingstoke: Palgrave Macmillan.

Faulkner, Guy, Raktim Mitra, Ron Buliung, Caroline Fusco and Michelle Stone. 2015. "Children's outdoor playtime, physical activity, and parental perceptions of the neighbourhood environment." *International Journal of Play* 4(1):84–97.

Ferber, Richard. 2006 (1985). *Solve Your Child's Sleep Problems.* New York: Fireside.

Fox, Bonnie. 2009. *When Couples Become Parents: The Creation of Gender in the Transition to Parenthood.* Toronto: University of Toronto Press.

Fréchette, Sabrina and Elisa Romano. 2015. "Change in corporal punishment over time in a representative sample of Canadian parents." *Journal of Family Psychology* 29(4):507–17.

Friendly, Martha, Bethany Grady, Lyndsay Macdonald and Barry Forer. 2015. "Early Childhood Education and Care in Canada 2014." Toronto: Childcare Resource and Research Unit.

Frønes, Ivar. 2009. "Childhood: Leisure, culture and peers." In *Palgrave Handbook of Childhood Studies*, edited by Jens Qvortrup, William A. Corsaro and Michael Sebastian Honig. Houndmills, Basingstoke: Palgrave Macmillan.

Furedi, Frank. 2002. *Paranoid Parenting: Why Ignoring the Experts May Be Best for Your Child.* Chicago: Chicago Review Press.

Ganann, Rebecca, Wendy Sword, Lehana Thabane, Bruce Newbold and Margaret Black. 2016. "Predictors of postpartum depression among immigrant women in the year after childbirth." *Journal of Women's Health* 25(2):155–65.

Glenn, Nicole M., Camilla J. Knight, Nicholas L. Holt and John C. Spence. 2012. "Meanings of play among children." *Childhood* 20(2):185–99.

Gopnik, Alison. 2016. *The Gardener and the Carpenter*. New York: Farrar, Straus and Giroux.

Grierson, Bruce. 2016. "How could you? When parent shaming goes too far." In *The Walrus*. Toronto: Walrus Foundation. December.

Guldberg, Helene. 2009. *Reclaiming Childhood: Freedom and Play in an Age of Fear*. London and New York: Routledge.

Gulli, Cathy. 2017. "The collapse of parenting: Why it's time for parents to grow up." In *Maclean's*. Toronto: Rogers Media. Jan. 7.

Hardyment, Christina. 1983. *Dream Babies: Child Care from Locke to Spock*. London: Jonathan Cape.

Hays, Sharon. 1996. *The Cultural Contradictions of Motherhood*. New Haven: Yale University Press.

Herrington, Susan and Mariana Brussoni. 2015. "Beyond physical activity: The importance of play and nature-based play spaces for children's health and development." *Current Obesity Reports* 4: 477–83.

Hoffman, Diane M. 2010. "Parenting and the production of the 'resilient child.'" *Health, Risk & Society* 12(4):385–94.

Honoré, Carl. 2008. *Under Pressure: Rescuing our Children from the Culture of Hyper-Parenting*. New York: HarperCollins.

Hunt, Alan. 2003. "Risk and moralization in everyday life." In *Risk and Morality*, edited by Richard V. Ericson and Aaron Doyle. Toronto: University of Toronto Press.

Hurley, Katie. 2015. *The Happy Kid Handbook: How to Raise Joyful Children in a Stressful World*. New York: Tarcher/Penguin.

Kadane, Lisa. 2013. "School's out: What happens to a community when students leave their neighbourhood schools?" In *Calgary Herald*. Calgary: Postmedia Network Inc. Nov. 8.

Kanieski, Mary Ann. 2010. "Securing attachment: The shifting medicalisation of attachment and attachment disorders." *Health, Risk & Society* 12(4):335–44.

Knaak, Stephanie. 2005. "Breast-feeding, bottle-feeding and Dr. Spock: The shifting context of choice." *Canadian Review of Sociology and Anthropology* 42(2):197–216.

—. 2009. "'Having a tough time': Towards an understanding of the psycho-social causes of postpartum emotional distress." *Journal of the Association for Research on Mothering* 11(1):80–94.

Lanes, Andrea, Jennifer L. Kuk and Hala Tamim. 2011. "Prevalence and characteristics of postpartum depression symptomatology among Canadian women: a cross-sectional study." *BMC Public Health* 11: 302(302).

Lauster, Nathanael. 2016. *The Death and Life of the Single-Family House: Lessons from Vancouver on Building a Livable City.* Philadelphia: Temple University Press.

Lee, Catherine M., Philip B. Smith, Susan B. Stern, Geneviève Piché, Steven Feldgaier, Christine Ateah, Marie-Eve Clément, Marie-Hélène Gagné, Annie Lamonde, Sue Barnes, and Diane Denis. 2014. "The international parenting survey-Canada: Exploring access to parenting services." *Canadian Psychology* 55(2):110–16.

Lee, Ellie. 2014. "Introduction." In *Parenting Culture Studies*, edited by Ellie Lee, Jennie Bristow, Charlotte Faircloth and Jan Macvarish. Houndmills, Basingstoke: Palgrave Macmillan.

Lee, Ellie, Jennie Bristow, Charlotte Faircloth and Jan Macvarish. 2014. *Parenting Culture Studies.* Houndmills, Basingstoke: Palgrave Macmillan.

Lewchuk, Wayne, Michelynn Lafleche, Stephanie Procyk, Charlene Cook, Diane Dyson, Luin Goldring, Karen Lior, Alan Meisner, John Shields, Anthony Tambureno, and Peter Viducis. 2015. "The Precarity Penalty." Toronto: McMaster University Social Sciences and United Way Toronto.

Liegghio, Maria. 2015. "Over 1000 aluminium cans for forty dollars: The provisioning contributions of older children from the perspectives of welfare-reliant lone mothers." *Children & Society* 29:388–98.

Loebach, Janet E. and Jason A. Gilliland. 2016. "Free range kids? Using GPS-derived activity spaces to examine children's neighborhood activity and mobility." *Environment and Behavior* 48(3):421–53.

Louv, Richard. 2008. *Last Child in the Woods: Saving our Children from Nature-Deficit Disorder.* Chapel Hill: Algonquin Books.

Luxton, Meg and June Corman. 2001. *Getting By in Hard Times: Gendered Labour at Home and on the Job.* Toronto: University of Toronto Press.

Macvarish, Jan. 2016. *Neuroparenting: The Expert Invasion of Family Life.* London: Palgrave Macmillan.

Malacrida, Claudia. 2007. "Negotiating the dependency/nurturance tightrope: Dilemmas of motherhood and disability." *Canadian Review of Sociology and Anthropology* 44(4):469–93.

McDonald, David and Martha Friendly. 2016. "A growing concern: 2016 child care fees in Canada's big cities." Ottawa: Canadian Centre for Policy Alternatives.

McKay, Lindsey, Sophie Mathieu and Andrea Doucet. 2016. "Parental-leave rich and parental-leave poor: Inequality in Canadian labour market based leave policies." *Journal of Industrial Relations* 58(4):543–62.

McKnight, John and Peter Block. 2010. *The Abundant Community: Awakening the Power of Families and Neighborhoods.* San Francisco: Berrett-Koehler Publishers Inc.

McLaren, Arlene Tigar 2016. "Families and transportation: Moving towards multimodality and altermobility?" *Journal of Transport Geography* 51:218–25.

McLaren, Arlene Tigar and Sylvia Parusel. 2015. "'Watching like a hawk': Gendered parenting in automobilized urban spaces." *Gender, Place and Culture* 22(10):1426–44.

McNamara, Lauren. 2013. "What's getting in the way of play? An analysis of the contextual factors that hinder recess in elementary schools." *Canadian Journal of Action Research* 14(2):3–21.

Mintz, Steven. 2004. *Huck's Raft: A History of American Childhood.* Cambridge MA: Bellknap Press.

Mose, Tamara R. 2016. *The Playdate: Parents, Children and the New Expectations of Play.* New York: New York University Press.

Nelson, Margaret K. 2010. *Parenting Out of Control: Anxious Parents in Uncertain Times.* New York: New York University Press.

Neufeld, Gordon and Gabor Maté 2013. *Hold on to Your Kids: Why Parents Need to Matter More than Peers.* Toronto: Vintage Canada.

Pace, Eric. 1998. "Benjamin Spock, world's pediatrician, dies at 94." In *The New York Times.* New York: The New York Times Company. March 17.

Parsons Leigh, Jeanna. 2016. "Skilled immigrants and the negotiation of family relations during settlement in Calgary, Alberta." *International Migration and Integration* 17: 1065–1083.

Pickert, Katie. 2012. "The man who remade motherhood." In *Time*. New York: Time Inc. May 12.

Ponzetti Jr, James. J. 2016. "Overview and history of parenting education." In *Evidence-Based Parenting Education: A Global Perspective*, edited by James J. Ponzetti Jr. New York: Routledge.

Premji, Stéphanie. 2017. "Precarious employment and difficult daily commutes." *Relations industrielles/Industrial Relations* 72(1):77–98.

Quirke, Linda. 2006. "'Keeping young minds sharp': Children's cognitive stimulation and the rise of parenting magazines, 1959–2003." *Canadian Review of Sociology and Anthropology* 43(4):387–406.

Ramaekers, Stefan and Judith Suissa. 2012. "What all parents need to know? Exploring the hidden normativity of the language of developmental psychology in parenting." *Journal of Philosophy of Education* 46(3):352–69.

Ranson, Gillian. 2010. *Against the Grain: Couples, Gender and the Reframing of Parenting*. Toronto: University of Toronto Press.

—. 2015. *Fathering, Masculinity and the Embodiment of Care*. Houndmills, Basingstoke: Palgrave Macmillan.

Rashi, Corinne, Trinity Wittman, Argerie Tsimicalis, and Carmen G. Loiselle. 2015. "Balancing illness and parental demands: coping with cancer while raising minor children." *Oncology Nursing Forum* 42(4):337–44.

Reece, Helen. 2013. "The pitfalls of positive parenting." *Ethics and Education* 8(1):42–54.

Rippeyoung, Phyllis L.F. 2013a. "Governing motherhood: Who pays and who profits?" Ottawa: Canadian Centre for Policy Alternatives.

—. 2013b. "Can breastfeeding solve inequality? The relative mediating impact of breastfeeding and home environment on poverty gaps in Canadian child cognitive skills." *Canadian Journal of Sociology* 38(1):65-85.

Russell, Alex with Tim Falconer. 2012. *Drop the Worry Ball: How to Parent in the Age of Entitlement*. Mississauga: John Wiley and Sons Canada.

Russell, Nancy Ukai. 2015. "Babywearing in the age of the internet." *Journal of Family Issues* 36(9):1130–53.

Sanders, Matthew R. and Karen M. Turner. 2016. "Triple P – Positive Parenting Program." In *Evidence-Based Parenting Education: A Global Perspective*, edited by James J. Ponzetti Jr. New York: Routledge.

Sax, Leonard. 2016. *The Collapse of Parenting: How We Hurt Our Kids When We Treat Them Like Grown-Ups*. New York: Basic Books.

Sears, William, Martha Sears, Robert Sears and James Sears. 2013. *The Baby Book: Everything You Need to Know About Your Baby from Birth to Age Two*. New York: Little, Brown and Company.

Sears, William and Martha Sears. 2001. *The Attachment Parenting Book: A Commonsense Guide to Understanding and Nurturing Your Baby*. New York: Little, Brown and Company.

Senior, Jennifer. 2014. *All Joy and No Fun: The Paradox of Modern Parenthood*. New York: HarperCollins.

Skenazy, Lenore. 2009. *Free-Range Kids: Giving our Children the Freedom We Had Without Going Nuts with Worry*. San Francisco: Jossey-Bass.

Spock, Benjamin. 1979. *Baby and Child Care*. New York: Pocket Books.

Stueck, Wendy. 2017. "Vancouver man ordered to stop letting his children take city bus to school." In *Globe and Mail*. Toronto: Woodbridge Company. Sept. 5

Tchoukaleyska, Roza. 2011. "Co-housing childhoods: Parents' mediation of urban risk through participation in intentional communities." *Children's Geographies* 9(2):235–46.

Thomas, Ashley J., P. Kyle Stanford and Barbara W. Sarnecka. 2016. "No child left alone: Moral judgments about parents affect estimates of risk to parents." *Collabra* 2(1)(10):1–14.

Thompson, Grace E., Rose E. Cameron and Esme Fuller-Thomson. 2012. "Achieving balance on the Red Road: First Nations grandparents speak." *Transition* Summer 3:6. Ottawa: Vanier Institute of the Family.

Thornton, Davi Johnson. 2011. "Neuroscience, affect and the entrepreneurialization of motherhood." *Communication and Critical/Cultural Studies* 8(4):399–424.

Torres, Juan. 2009. "Children & Cities: Planning to Grow Together." Ottawa: Vanier Institute of the Family.

Tremblay, Mark S., Casey Gray, Shawna Babcock, Joel Barnes, Christa Costas Bradstreet, Dawn Carr, Guylaine Chabot, Louise Choquette, David Chorney, Cam Collyer, Susan Herrington, Katherine Janson, Ian Janssen, Richard Larouche, William Pickett, Marlene Power, Ellen Beate Hansen Sandseter, Brenda Simon, and Mariana Brussoni. 2015. "Position Statement on Active Outdoor Play." *International Journal of Environmental Research and Public Health* 12:6475–505.

Tuteur, Amy. 2016. *Push Back: Guilt in the Age of Natural Parenting*. New York: HarperCollins.

Valenti, Jessica. 2012. *Why Have Kids? A New Mom Explores the Truth about Parenting and Happiness*. Boston: Houghton Mifflin Harcourt.

VanderPlaat, Madine, Howard Ramos, and Yoko Yoshida. 2012. "What do sponsored parents and grandparents contribute?" *Canadian Ethnic Studies* 44(3):79–96.

Wall, Glenda. 2004. "'Is your child's brain maximized?': Mothering in an age of new brain research." *Atlantis* 28(2):41–50.

—. 2010. "Mothers' experiences with intensive parenting and brain development discourse." *Women's Studies International Forum* 33:253–63.

—. 2013. "'Putting family first': Shifting discourses of motherhood and childhood in representations of mothers' employment and child care." *Women's Studies International Forum* 40: 162–171.

—. Forthcoming. "'Love builds brains': Representations of attachment and children's brain development in parenting education material." *Sociology of Health and Illness*.

Whalen, Heather and Glen Schmidt. 2016. "The women who remain behind: Challenges in the LDC lifestyle." *Rural Society* 25(1):1–14.

Wilson, Philip, Robert Rush, Susan Hussey, Christine Puckering, Fiona Sim, Clare S. Allely, Paul Doku, Alex McConnachie and Christopher Gillberg. 2012. "How evidence-based is an 'evidence-based parenting program'? A PRISMA systematic review and meta-analysis of Triple P." *BMC Medicine* 10: 130.

Woodhead, Martin. 2009. "Child development and the development of childhood." In *Palgrave Handbook of Childhood Studies*, edited by Jens Qvortrup, William A. Corsaro and Michael-Sebastian Honig. Houndmills, Basingstoke: Palgrave Macmillan.

Zhou, Yanqui R. 2013. "Toward transnational care interdependence: Rethinking the relationships between care, immigration and social policy." *Global Social Policy* 13(3):280–98.

Zilio, Michele. 2017. "Ottawa signs child-care deal targeting families in need." In *Globe and Mail*. Toronto: Woodbridge Company. June 12.

Index

172
support 42, 56, 59, 63,
  118–121.
  and community agen-
  cies 62, 63, 91
  and social media 32,
  34, 42, 63, 89–90, 118,
  119
  from friends and other
  family 61, 91, 118, 119
  lack of/isolation 120
surveillance 57, 96–97,
  116–117, 132, 133
  see also grandparents

T

Thomas, Ashley 134,
  153, 161, 173
time use by children
  and child care 86
  down time 105, 121
  structured activities
  87, 104–106
  time outdoors 122, 132
  see also play
  see also screen time
Today's Parent 16, 17,
  31, 34, 158
Torres, Juan 44, 159, 173
trajectories of caring 61,
  70
Tuteur, Amy 28–29, 162,
  173

V

Valenti, Jessica 127, 161,
  174
Vanier Institute of the
  Family 148, 165, 167,
  173

W

Wall, Glenda 6, 16, 17,
  19, 129, 154, 155, 161,
  174

Woodhead, Martin 130,
  161, 174
work-family balance 39,
  99
  and gender 39
  and government policy
  148

Y

Yummy Mummy Club
  30, 31